BAJA CALIFORNIA MISSIONS

The Southwest Center Series

Joseph C. Wilder, Editor

BAJA CALIFORNIA MISSIONS

In the Footsteps of the Padres

TEXT BY

David Burckhalter

PHOTOGRAPHS BY DAVID BURCKHALTER AND MINA SEDGWICK

FOREWORD BY BERNARD L. FONTANA

THE UNIVERSITY OF ARIZONA PRESS

TUCSON

THE UNIVERSITY OF
ARIZONA PRESS

www.uapress.arizona.edu

Burckhalter, David L.
Baja California missions : in the footsteps of the padres / text by David Burckhalter; photographs by David Burckhalter and Mina Sedgwick ; foreword by Bernard L. Fontana. Includes bibliographical references and index.
pages cm. — (The Southwest Center series)
ISBN 978-0-8165-2119-7 (pbk. : alk. paper) 1. Spanish mission buildings—Mexico—Baja California (Peninsula) I. Title.
NA5256.B3B87 2013
726.50972'2—dc23
2012041270

Church floor plans adapted by Jim Sauer from *Misiones en la Pen de Baja California*, José Luis Aguilar Marco, et al, 1991 and *Las Misiones Antiguas*, Edward W. Vernon, 2002

Manufactured in South Korea on acid-free, archival-quality paper and processed chlorine free.

18 17 16 15 14 13 6 5 4 3 2 1

Contents

Dedicated to
the padres and the indigenous people of Baja, California:
gone forever.

Illustrations

Foreword

In recent years there have been growing numbers of books whose subject matter is the churches and associated structures built in northern New Spain under the auspices of Jesuit, Franciscan, and Dominican religious orders. In addition to detailed surveys, such as that of Gloria Giffords, *Sanctuaries of Earth, Stone and Light* (Tucson: University of Arizona Press, 2007), and another compiled by Clara Bargellini and Michael Komanecky, *The Arts of the Missions of Northern New Spain* (Mexico City: Antigua Colegio de San Ildefonso, 2009), there have been illustrated volumes focusing on individual churches or groups of churches in, for example, California and New Mexico.

One region of northern New Spain, however, has received less attention than the others. It is that of peninsular Baja California, both the separate states of Baja California Norte and Baja California Sur. Only Edward Vernon's comprehensive *Las Misiones Antiguas: The Spanish Missions of Baja California* (Santa Barbara, CA: Viejo Press, 2002) affords a recent overview of these unlikely missions, one that includes not only standing structures but ruins as well. Bárbara Meyer de Stinglhamber's *Arte sacro en Baja California Sur—siglos XVII–XIX* (Mexico City: Instituto Nacional de Antropología e Historia, 2001), which does not consider missions in Baja California Norte, has not been translated into English, is not easily obtainable, and is avowedly a catalog of church artifacts rather than a volume intended to give its readers a sense of the places with which these artifacts were, and in some cases still are, associated.

Photographer/writer David Burckhalter and photographer Mina Sedgwick have elected to focus on the eight still-standing Spanish-period stone churches in Baja California, two of them in Baja California Norte and six in Baja California Sur. Via words and visual imagery the reader is guided on an armchair journey through some of the most beautiful desert country of northwestern Mexico, given a glimpse at the history of the region, and afforded an introduction to places and people comparatively unknown to those of us who live beyond the region. Setting, history, architecture, and art come together in the pages of this book, along with the realization that these places continue to be an integral part of the social and religious fabric of the communities where they are found.

Baja California Missions is sure to rank high among books about Spanish missions and about California's southerly peninsula neighbor. The contribution is a welcome one.

Bernard L. Fontana

Preface

I've spent a good amount of time during the last four decades photographing and writing about Native Americans of Sonora, Mexico, especially the Seri Indians (Comcaac), who live in the desert by the Sea of Cortés (Gulf of California). When I camped on the beach near the Seri village of Desemboque in the early days, I used to watch the sun go down over the sea with mysterious Baja California outlined on the horizon, wondering what it would be like to go there.

The Seri have a legend that their ancestors were a race of giants who came across the sea from Baja California to settle on the Sonora coast. Only one hundred years ago, Seri fishermen and their families still paddled back and forth from the mainland across the narrow Infiernillo Strait to Tiburón Island on *balsas*, elongated rafts made from three bundled shafts of *carrizo*, or freshwater reeds. Seri mariners of old used balsas to island hop across the central gulf to Baja California.

I finally did travel to the peninsula in the 1980s, taking the car ferry across the sea from Guaymas to Santa Rosalía. I went there to photograph the strange, wonderful plants of the central desert, boojums and elephant trees. Though many years have gone by since then, Baja's magic spell was cast upon me. I knew that one day I would return.

The idea to create a book about the missions of Mexico's Baja California emerged during a journey to the peninsula in the spring of 2006. Mina (Guillermina Arenas) Sedgwick and I embarked on a two-week road trip from Tucson, Arizona, driving the 800-mile length of a landmass that Spanish explorers once considered an island. With a mutual interest in Spanish colonial churches of Mexico, we decided to visit a number of historic missions during our sojourn. About halfway down Baja's Transpeninsular Highway, we turned onto the dirt track that led to San Francisco de Borja Adac, a mission I had seen twenty years before while taking photographs in the lush desert of the area. The road to the mission was terribly jolting and dusty but worth it just for the spectacular scenery. On a plateau in the middle of nowhere, surrounded by desert and mountains, stood the stunning eighteenth-century Spanish church of San Francisco de Borja, a beige-colored stone building that glowed in *luz amarilla*, the yellow light of sundown.

Continuing our trip through central Baja, we introduced ourselves to the towering mission church at the San Ignacio oasis and to the impressive historic Christian temples at Mulegé and Loreto by the Sea of Cortés. Just south of Loreto we motored over the Sierra de la Giganta to Misión San Javier. The eighteenth-century San Javier church was a revelation to us because of its majestic setting, magnificent stone architecture, and gilded altars, vibrant paintings, and sculpture. On the cape at the southern end of the peninsula, we visited rebuilt mission churches at La Paz, Santiago, Todos Santos, and San José del Cabo. These modern buildings, though attractive, lacked the presence and charm of original churches. Returning to northern Baja California, we reconnoitered the two ruined missions of San Fernando and the sites at Rosario and Santo Domingo. These locations (along with seventeen other missions in total ruin) held little interest for us, displaying only historical markers and plastered-over adobe walls.

On the way back home, Mina and I discussed creating a book of photographs about the Baja California missions. From what we had seen, it made sense to focus on just the architecture and art of the historic intact eighteenth-century Spanish churches. There were eight of these mission churches, all of them built with stone. The five missions we had seen during our reconnaissance, Nuestra Señora de Loreto Conchó, San Francisco Javier Viggé Biaundó, Santa Rosalía de Mulegé, San Ignacio de Kadakaamán, and San Francisco de Borja Adac, beckoned to us to return for thorough, reflective photography. Thoughts of exploring the three remaining missions we hadn't seen, San José de Comondú, San Luis Gonzaga Chiriyaqui, and Santa Gertrudis de Cadacamán, set our plans in motion for future adventures across the wilds of Baja.

During the considerable time we spent driving across Baja California, Mina and I never tired of looking at dazzling landscapes as we sped through mountains and endless desert and along the coasts. Most of all, we loved examining the churches and religious art up close. Usually we were the only ones there. The best part of traveling to the missions a second and third time was discovering things we missed before. We enjoyed most the isolated churches that were hard to get to. We'd camp out for a couple of days and then treat ourselves to a nice hotel room, a bottle of wine, a good dinner. It was great fun talking with the locals wherever we went. There were some agonizing moments: wondering if we were lost on the back roads; getting low on gas; navigating treacherous Mexico Highway #1 with huge transport trucks bearing down on us from the opposite direction; looking for a motel late at night. We drove Mina's Ford Expedition, a great vehicle for highway driving, for the worst of dirt roads, and for camping on a moment's notice.

On our second trip to Baja California, after photographing at Misión San Ignacio and spending a night in the upscale La Pinta Hotel in the town of San Ignacio, Mina and I drove north, leaving civilization and the paved highway for unknown dirt roads that would take us to Misión Santa Gertrudis. Until we reached our destination, we saw absolutely no one in two hours of relentless pounding across the faceless desert. Beyond the halfway point to the mission, the road wended its way into an area thick with large mesquite trees. A little white dog jumped out of the brush and took off after us, hightailing it for several miles. It just kept running and running. As we passed a deserted ranch house, the dog turned into the yard and stayed. Mina felt sad not to have stopped to give such a loyal companion food and water. We looked for the abandoned dog on the way back, but it wasn't there.

The lovely stone church at Santa Gertrudis commands a fine view across its broad, low canyon. The handful of people who lived there were friendly and extremely trusting. They let us explore and photograph the church at will. We were moved by the kindness of a couple employed as caretakers of an estate with orchards and fields. They offered us a suite in the small hacienda, welcomed us for conversation, and fed us dinner and breakfast, asking nothing in return. Wandering the date palm groves, dense foliage, and tranquil pools of the lonely arroyo below the church, we felt the natural wildness and total isolation of the place, virtually unchanged since missionary times.

On our third visit to Santa Rosalía de Mulegé, Mina and I hoped to rephotograph the church exterior, main gallery, and altar. When we arrived at the church, we saw pickup trucks, scaffolding, wooden planks, and paint drums scattered about the parking lot: the site had become a construction zone. Drop cloths hung down over the church gallery; plaster was splattered across the plastic floor covering; workmen buzzed about. Along came the grinning construction crew chief, who told us he had labored eighteen years restoring the historic churches of Baja California Sur. He showed off the freshly completed, whitewashed side chapel, where we found the lovely original eighteenth-century wooden statue of Santa Rosalía, absent on our previous trips, out of storage and on display.

At San José de Comondú, on our second trip there, we intended to take a few more interior photographs, especially of the main altar. That proved impossible, as remodeling was going on around the altar, and the San José and Santa María statues had disappeared from their stations. We noticed that the oil paintings of various saints hanging on opposing walls of the chapel, stained, tarnished, and several of them perforated with gaping holes on our first visit two years earlier, now glistened like new, having been completely restored. After we asked the amiable caretaker of San José de Comondú where the missing altar statues were being kept during the remodeling, he invited us into his home. The eighteenth-century statues of San José and Santa María stood side by side atop his wife's dresser against a salmon-colored bedroom wall, a perfect backdrop for taking close-up photographs!

Our second-favorite Baja California mission church—after stunning San Francisco de Borja Adac—was awe-inspiring San Javier. Mina and I visited San Javier a third time to attend the annual saint's day celebration on December 3. The San Javier church was crowded daily with pilgrims and celebrants, the four-day carnival being in full swing. During the saint's procession, I was surprised by the appearance of the *matachines*, festival dancers in colorful regalia that evoke Indian Mexico before the conquest. Matachines usually dance to celebrate the Virgin of Guadalupe or a patron saint, in this case, San Francisco Javier. Besides observing and photographing the religious activities, we totally enjoyed the fiesta, spending two nights camping in an orchard below the church.

Mina and I took the photographs for this book during our last two trips to Baja California, in March 2007 and December 2009. We made certain to request permission from the authorities or resident caretaker to take photographs inside each church. The majority of our images were recorded with handheld Canon EOS 30D digital SLR cameras. We preferred natural interior lighting, a tripod occasionally being brought to the rescue for certain low-light shots. Since no restrictions were posted prohibiting flash photography, we did use flash illumination.

In the book's narrative, I've used the word "mission" in several ways. "Mission," the "old mission," or a specific name, "Misión San Francisco de Borja Adac," for example, refers to the particular church building erected by colonizing Roman Catholic priests. The word "mission" also names and alludes to the agrarian colony, the church being its focal point, which included living quarters for the clergy, Indian converts, and Spanish colonists, as well as communal buildings, open public areas, orchards, planted fields, corrals, and pastureland. A "mission," in the broader sense, proclaims the quest of the padres to spread the Holy Spirit into the world by converting "godless heathens" to Christianity.

Acknowledgments

I wish to thank Mina Sedgwick for being the perfect Baja California traveling companion, for her ideas, and for contributing twelve terrific photographs to this book. I am grateful to Jeff Banister, who read the manuscript at different stages, offering enthusiasm and thoughtful input. I thank Bunny Fontana and three anonymous scholars, who gave much of themselves to offer valuable suggestions for improving the text. Their positive criticism and corrections provided needed guidance. Paul Mirocha created a great map of Baja California, one that highlights topography, major highways, and important towns and locates the Spanish mission sites. Jim Sauer drew the excellent church floor plans.

To Dianne Bret Harte and the Southwestern Foundation, I say *¡mil gracias!* Without Dianne's blessing and the Southwestern Foundation's financial support in the form of two generous grants, this book would have been impossible to complete. Thanks to Joe Wilder at the University of Arizona's Southwest Center for additional financial aid and for placing the book in the Southwest Center Book Series. I salute Allyson Carter, my acquiring editor at the University of Arizona Press, for committing to the long journey of seeing the book through to publication.

Finally, I tip my hat to the gracious, hardy folk of Baja California, whose task it will be to continue cherishing and protecting the Spanish colonial mission churches, architectural treasures that embody their own illustrious heritage.

David Burckhalter, Tucson, Arizona
November 2011

BAJA CALIFORNIA MISSIONS

Baja California with Spanish Colonial Mission Sites
Intact eighteenth-century churches
Modern rebuilt churches
Churches in ruins
0 10 20 30 40 50 miles
ARIZONA
UNITED STATES
MEXICO
SONORA
SINALOA
BAJA CALIFORNIA NORTE
BAJA CALIFORNIA SUR
PACIFIC OCEAN
Gulf of California
(Sea of Cortés)
San Diego
Tijuana
Tecate
Mexicali
Yuma
San Luis Río Colorado
Río Colorado
Tucson
Nogales
Nogales
Puerto Peñasco
San Felipe
Hermosillo
Río Sonora
Guaymas
Río Yaqui
Ciudad Obregón
Río Mayo
El Descanso
Guadalupe
San Miguel
Santa Catalina
Ensenada
Santo Tomás
San Vicente
Santo Domingo
San Pedro Mártir
San Quintín
Rosario
El Rosario
San Fernando
Santa Maria
Cataviña
Calamajué
Isla Angel de la Guarda
Isla Tiburón
Bahía de los Angeles
San Borja
Rosarito
Isla Cedros
El Arco
Guerrero Negro
Santa Gertrudis
San Pablo
Bahía Tortugas
LAS TRES VIRGINES
Santa Rosalía
San Ignacio
San Ignacio
Guadalupe Guasinapí
Mulegé
Mulegé
La Purísima
Londó
San Bruno
San José de Comondú
San Miguel de Comondú
Loreto
Loreto
San Javier
La Presentación
Liguí
Villa Insurgentes
Ciudad Constitución
Dolores Apaté
La Pasión
San Luis Gonzaga
La Paz
La Paz
Santa Rosa
Todos Santos
Santiago
Santiago
San José del Cabo
San José del Cabo
Cabo San Lucas
SIERRA DE JUAREZ
SIERRA SAN PEDRO MARTIR
SIERRA SAN BORJA
SIERRA DE SAN FRANCISCO
SIERRA DE LA GIGANTA
SIERRA DE LA LAGUNA
N

The Setting

Baja California Geography

Fresh water has always been the critical element for survival on Baja California. Peninsular Native Americans needed to keep close to permanent waterholes during their search for food. When the Roman Catholic priests arrived, they too needed enduring springs by which to base their operations, to work the magic of creating mission oases. Even today, the presence of water or its absence affects Baja California's population distribution. As a modern aspect of dealing with Baja's chronic lack of fresh water, Mexican hydrology engineers focus on fresh technologies: desalinization, water recycling through filtration purification, and continued deep water drilling.

The Baja California peninsula, containing a land area of 56,000 square miles, stretches nearly 800 miles in a southeasterly direction from the US–Mexico border at San Diego–Tijuana to its southernmost point at Finisterra, Land's End, at Cabo San Lucas. Baja's thin finger of desert and mountain terrain separates the Gulf of California (Sea of Cortés) from the Pacific Ocean and spreads from east to west across distances varying from 125 to 25 miles. Another peninsula by way of comparison is the state of Florida, located on the southeastern seaboard of North America, which contains 66,000 square miles of territory, 10,000 more than Baja, and separates the northern part of the Gulf of Mexico from the Atlantic Ocean. Florida's thumb-shaped lowland peninsula extends south for 450 miles, 350 miles less than the length of Baja California.

Geologically, Baja California was originally part of the North American Plate, the tectonic plate to which

Mexico has remained attached. Five million years ago, the peninsula began taking shape as the East Pacific Rise undercut the margin of the North American Plate, creating over time a huge slice of earth, separating it from the Mexican mainland. As the peninsula forced itself west into the Pacific Ocean, the Gulf of California opened between the peninsula and the mainland. This gradual undercutting action and the separation of tectonic plates continue today. Presently, the mouth of the gulf gapes across 150 miles of open sea.

Underground fissures continue to split northward up through the Colorado River delta and across the Salton Sea and Imperial Valley of southern California. These actively shifting land rifts, the San Andreas Fault being one of them, pass by Los Angeles and through the western San Joaquin Valley, all the way north to the San Francisco Bay. The silting of the Colorado River and its delta actually holds back the Gulf of California, keeping it from flooding below-sea-level locations like Mexicali in Baja California and the Imperial Valley of California. Baja California, now part of the Pacific Plate, continues to move away from the East Pacific Rise in a northwesterly direction.

The Baja peninsula is divided at the twenty-eighth parallel into Mexican states of almost equal size, Baja California (Norte) and Baja California Sur, the two regions achieving statehood in 1953 and 1974. Mexicali is the capital of Baja Norte, while La Paz is the capital of Baja Sur. Baja California is sparsely populated over most of its rural territory. Seventy-five percent of Baja California Norte's three million people live in Tijuana, Ensenada, and Mexicali. The majority of Baja California Sur's half-million residents live around the cape region, in La Paz, Todos Santos, San José del Cabo, and Cabo San Lucas. Tourism, export manufacturing, real estate, ranching, and agriculture provide the main economic resources of the Baja California peninsula.

The highest point on the peninsula is found in Baja Norte at El Picacho del Diablo of the Sierra San Pedro Mártir, a peak that crests at nearly 10,000 feet. In the center of Baja California spreads the Vizcaíno Biosphere Reserve, the largest, most diverse protected area in Latin America. It includes the Vizcaíno Desert and the Pacific Ocean gray whale breeding waters of Laguna Ojo de Liebre (Scammon's Lagoon) near the town of Guerrero Negro and locations farther south at Laguna San Ignacio and Bahía Magdalena. Other important mountain ranges lie in Baja California Sur: Sierra de San Francisco; Tres Virgenes volcanic peaks; the extensive Sierra de la Giganta, which parallels the Gulf of California coast for 125 miles. In the cape region south of La Paz, the Sierra de la Laguna reach over 7,000 feet.

Most of Baja California belongs to the Sonoran Desert ecosystem, with the exception of a Mediterranean-like climate area around Tijuana and Ensenada and inland to wine country and part of the cape that exhibits subtropical affinities with Sinaloa on the Mexican mainland. Baja California comprises 45 percent of the Sonoran Desert's territory. The Sonoran Desert, which also traverses parts of Arizona, California, and Sonora, Mexico, is the hottest desert in North America, unique in its array of specialized animals and xerophytic cacti and woody plants. The Baja California peninsula possesses an extremely variable climate. Temperatures over the land can change 45 degrees Fahrenheit in a twenty-four-hour period. Annual rainfall varies some years from 0 inches in the desert to 48 inches in the mountains. Winter rain produced over the Pacific Ocean falls on the western mountain slopes but, due to the rain-shadow effect, does not reach the eastern, leeward slopes. Summer rains originate in weather systems created over the tropics. Sometimes these tropical systems generate tremendous hurricanes that bring periodic destruction across the peninsula.

The climate is highly sensitive to the surrounding marine environment. On Baja California's west coast, the windblown Pacific Ocean side is regulated by the cold California Current coming down the North American continent from the subarctic northern Pacific. This current, together with strong winds, creates cool temperatures, sending clouds and fog off the water and over the desert. In the central desert, fog brings life-giving moisture to hard-pressed plants and animals. The protected Gulf of California side of the peninsula, by contrast, receives warm water from the tropical southern Pacific Ocean (10 degrees Fahrenheit warmer than the open Pacific). The gulf's surface is also warmed because of its shallow depths, particularly in the upper gulf, causing evaporation and higher salinity and raising dry air temperatures over the land.

Introduction

They appear suddenly, coming into view seemingly out of nowhere, each one an extraordinary structure that dominates its surroundings. They are the eight surviving original Spanish colonial missions of Baja California. It's a miracle these eighteenth-century churches exist at all: three of them are virtually lost in the desert, two are secluded in the mountains, three anchor towns that have grown up around or near them. Two of the stone churches are majestic, with soaring towers and domes, exquisite façades, huge arched windows that allow the play of sunlight across vast interior spaces. Four churches are stunning because of their commanding presence and perfect placement on the land. Two are humble, even modest, churches that reflect purity and warmth in a minimalist approach to religious architecture. Due to the tragic extinction of the Indians for whom the missions were established, the eight surviving Spanish colonial churches, erected over two centuries ago, were abandoned just years after their completion. These once-deserted churches exist today because they were built of stone.

No one knows for certain exactly what happened to the eight churches after the Roman Catholic priests abandoned them in the early nineteenth century. The four greatest Christian churches of Baja California, churches that stood at the heart of the most successful missions, Nuestra Señora de Loreto, San Francisco Javier, San Ignacio, and San José, were probably never completely forsaken but were looked after by descendants of the colonists who stayed on to develop towns in place of the former missions. Perhaps that's why much of the eighteenth-century artwork and many written documents have been preserved at these four churches, sanctuaries that eventually came into regular service again. The most isolated stone churches of San

Francisco, Santa Gertrudis, San Luis Gonzaga, and Santa Rosalía near the Sea of Cortés coast have little original art and few church records to show. Mostly just the church buildings remain at these sites, evidence that these missions were totally deserted for long periods of time.

The history of Baja California's first colonizers, the indefatigable priests who founded the missions and built these astonishing stone churches, is a fascinating tale. Charged with religious fervor, Catholic priests of the Jesuit, Franciscan, and Dominican orders came to Baja California to change the cultural landscape, to create a new society. They established thirty-four Spanish missions on Mexico's Baja California peninsula from 1697 to 1834. Misión Nuestra Señora de Loreto Conchó, Baja's first Jesuit outpost, was founded on October 25, 1697. Loreto became the "cabeza y madre de las misiones de Baja y Alta California" (head and mother of the missions of Lower and Upper California). Baja California's missions were established to colonize and convert Native Americans to Christianity. Jesuit padres were the first to spread the faith across the peninsula. They corralled the Native American nomads and brought them to the missions for baptism and conversion. For seventy years the Jesuits organized the Indians to cultivate the land. They put them to the task of building beautiful churches.

After Charles III of Spain expelled the Jesuits in 1767, Baja California's colonization was taken over by Franciscans, then by Dominicans. These two succeeding Catholic orders founded missions and built churches of their own during the next sixty-seven years. Spanish colonists who immigrated to Baja California in the eighteenth century brought Old World diseases with them, infecting the indigenous people. With no natural immunity against the pestilences, the Indians of Baja California quickly began to die off. By 1840 smallpox epidemics had caused the extinction of three of Baja's four tribes, the Cochimí, Guaycura, and Pericú. A few Yuman are today's only survivors of the fourth tribe. As a result of these decimations, all thirty-four Roman Catholic missions were abandoned. Now, 170 years later, eight stone churches are the only intact buildings left from the great Spanish colonization experience. While five modern churches have been rebuilt on or near the original mission sites, twenty-one of Baja California's Spanish churches, which were constructed of adobe and other ephemeral materials, have mostly crumbled back to the earth, vanishing like the Indians themselves.

Baja California's eight eighteenth-century stone churches stand resplendent today, thanks to forty years of painstaking structural reconstruction and delicate artwork restoration conducted under the direction of Mexico's Instituto Nacional de Antropología e Historia (INAH). Baja's churches endure as landmark monuments of Mexico's colonial legacy, important as well to the heritage of the southwestern United States. These splendid structures bear witness to the faith and zeal of the priests and to the toil of the Indians.

Each mission church on Baja California possessed an inventory of commissioned religious art created in the eighteenth-century workshops of central Mexico, beautiful objects shipped to the peninsula across the Gulf of California, lugged overland from the coast by pack animals. Many objects that remained inside the once-abandoned stone churches—written records and documents, books, sacred paraphernalia, communion chalices, woven vestments, baptismal fonts, furniture, musical instruments, bronze bells, gilded wooden altar screens, sculptures in wood and stone, oil paintings on canvas depicting the life of Jesus Christ and the saints, exceptional work by anonymous Mexican artists—have been archived and restored by the INAH, and some have been re-placed in situ.

Baja California was "discovered" in 1535 by Hernán Cortés, governor-general of Nueva España, or New Spain (Mexico). Cortés is best known as the conquistador, or conqueror, of the Aztec Empire in 1521. At the time of its discovery, California, as the Spanish first called the peninsula, was believed to be an island, a fallacy that persisted among many European geographers for two centuries. Due to its aridity, infertile land, incredible heat, and lack of fresh water and food, not to mention its menacing, warlike natives, Baja California was not colonized until 1697.

Fresh water provided by natural springs or water catchments afforded the major element to founding a mission in the Baja California desert—a place where an oasis could be created. A mission based on the rural Spanish colonial model, a self-sufficient farming village spread around its church, needed plenty of arable land and grazing to support a sizable Indian population. Arriving at the chosen spot, the priest, his small military escort, and Christianized Indians accompanying him first erected a ramada under which to hold religious services. Then they built temporary living, cooking, and dining quarters, sometimes enclosing the nascent encampment with a defensive stockade. Construction was primitive. The pioneers used frameworks of mesquite wood to support walls of *adobe y cañas*, wattle and daub, placing reeds or thatch over their structures for roofing. Eventually a formal church, priest's residence, dormitories for the unmarried, huts for married Indian families, and storage houses for food and farming equipment would be erected of sun-dried adobe bricks. Near to the mission would be built a presidio, a fort to house the military garrison. The construction of a permanent stone church, which replaced the adobe structure, occurred only at the most mature, successful missions. It took forty to fifty years beyond a mission's founding to finally build a stone church.

At the mission where they would devote their life's work, the padres introduced a signature plant, the Mediterranean date palm. They also brought to Baja California many crop plants (wheat, maize, citrus trees, grapes, sugarcane, figs, olives, and pomegranates) along with domestic farm animals (horses, donkeys, cattle, sheep, pigs, goats, and chickens). Some of Baja California's eight beautiful eighteenth-century stone churches, both monumental and humble, were financed by wealthy Spanish benefactors. Nearby stone quarries and readily available Indian workers were indispensable. To create beautiful buildings, the priests needed to import stonecutters and masons from Mexico.

The early colonization of Baja California was organized along theocratic lines. In the beginning, Jesuit priests commanded the Spanish military forces that accompanied them in the colonial enterprise. It took relentless grit, not to mention considerable political and financial maneuvering, for the Jesuits to embark on their unprecedented spiritual and territorial conquest. The founding Jesuit colonization program (and later efforts of the Franciscans and Dominicans) involved *reducción*, the process of gathering and moving widely scattered nomadic Native Americans and bringing them to mission settlements, where they could be controlled by the priests; *congregación*, the task of physically concentrating the wanderers to live communally as mission farmers and stock herders; and teaching them as *neófitos*—neophytes converted to Roman Catholicism—to live and work among *gente de razón*, people of reason, the neófitos' mentors in civilization, Europeans and Mexicans born into Christianity. At the center of the mission stood its church, the *templo de Dios* (God's temple), a majestic hall filled with sacred objects, a holy place where rites of passage were performed: baptism, conversion, affirmation, marriage, death, celebration. The important events of the converted Indians' lives now took place in and around the mission church.

When Jesuit priest Juan María de Salvatierra established the first lasting Spanish colony at Loreto, on the Gulf of California, in 1697, an estimated fifty thousand Native Americans roamed the coasts, deserts, and mountains of Baja California. It was a clash of cultures from the beginning. The Stone Age nomads that the priests and Spanish soldiers defeated, congregated, and converted were divided into four distinct cultural and linguistic groups. Having no affinity with Indians of mainland Mexico, except for the desert Seri of coastal Sonora, who practiced a similar lifestyle, the Cochimí, Guaycura, Pericú, and Yuman ranged over the 800-mile-long peninsula. The four tribes survived as hunters and gatherers of the desert and sea. Separate bands occupied separate territories, speaking different dialects of the four languages (Cochimí, Guaycura, Pericú, and Yuman). These Indians were by no means united among themselves, as they waged constant warfare on each other.

The Cochimí occupied the center of the peninsula, ranging north almost to the Colorado River. The Pericú were distributed across the cape at the southern tip of Baja California and also occupied offshore coastal islands. The Guaycura ranged in between the Cochimí and the Pericú, overlapping territories with both, competing for the same resources. The Yuman tribes lived in the north, from the Pacific coast across to the Colorado River delta. When the Jesuits were expelled from Baja California in 1768, approximately five thousand Indians remained in the Jesuit region of conquest; that is, in seventy years, 90 percent of the three southern tribes had already been decimated by smallpox, measles, typhus, influenza, and venereal disease. Diseases spread easily through the Baja California missions and with devastating effect due to unsanitary conditions created by the tightly packed communal living quarters. Pregnant women and newborn children were especially vulnerable, the first ones killed by pestilence. By 1800 the Guaycura and Pericú had become extinct, the more numerous Cochimí dying off by 1840. Only a few descendants of the Yuman survive today in northern Baja California.

The Cochimí, Guaycura, and Pericú bands that occupied the southern three-quarters of the peninsula possessed rudimentary technology, having minimal material culture. They hunted deer and bighorn sheep with bow and arrow, chasing down and clubbing smaller animals, and they harvested shellfish from the littoral and seized sea turtles from the shallows of the sea. They used the fire drill and chipped stone to fashion scrapers, knives, spears, bows, arrows, and projectile points. The Indians of Baja California practiced no agriculture and owned no domestic animals, not even dogs. They lived in semi-autonomous bands, several families coming together at temporary villages, called *rancherías* by the priests. They were attuned to seasonal movements based on the shifting geography of freshwater sources and coastal and desert plant harvests, celebrating especially during the abundant summertime the ripening of cactus fruits.

Always on the move, Baja California Indians had no fixed homes or portable shelters, scant clothing, and, with the exception of the Pericú, who made balsas or reed rafts, no boats. The Pericú also wove baskets and manufactured fired pottery for cooking and carrying water. Face painting was the primary adornment of the peninsula tribes. Fantastic cave paintings found in the mountains of central Baja California offer a prehistoric view of tribal ancestors. These brilliantly colored pictographs of human and animal forms were likely painted by Cochimí predecessors over one thousand years ago. Cochimí storytellers told the Jesuits that these ancestors came from a race of giants.

The indigenous people of Baja California were ruled by respected headmen and shamans, individuals the Jesuits called *hechiceros* (wizards or medicine men), powerful leaders who relied on visions for spiritual guidance. These Indian strongmen commonly practiced polygamy. The Jesuits were eternally frustrated by the independent nomads, who lacked the words to express European social perceptions, feelings, concepts, and everyday abstractions. Products of their own self-righteousness and conceit, the Jesuits learned little in return about the Indians. They strongly discouraged traditional practices, even the gathering of native foods. They never produced native-language dictionaries. Only padres Miguel del Barco and Juan Jacobo Baegert compiled ethnographic data, and they did so with specific objectives in mind that deeply colored their accounts. Detractors alleged that Jesuits held the natives in virtual slavery, that colonization meant genocide. And yet for mission Indians, the priests were their only defenders against unscrupulous gente de razón and rapacious Spanish soldiers who violated their women.

In the realm of religious architecture and art presented to the Indians, in stark contrast to the minimalist native way of life, Jesuit, Franciscan, and Dominican priests who built and decorated Baja California's beautiful churches were promoters of the *barroco,* or baroque, the flamboyant Roman Catholic artistic style that blossomed in Europe and the New World during the seventeenth and eighteenth centuries. Best seen on Baja California in the elaborate churches of San Francisco Javier Viggé Biaundó and San Ignacio de Kadakaamán, the baroque expressed spiritual joy with ornate façades and airy sunlit interior spaces. Closely linked with colonialism, baroque architecture appealed to the landed aristocracy, manifested in magnificent estates and public buildings that displayed triumphant power. The Jesuits believed pictorial art should communicate religious themes directly and with emotion. Characterized by dynamic movement and bright colors, baroque paintings and sculpture spoke to the illiterate masses with sensual appeal in understandable iconography that was both heroic and inspirational.

The Roman Catholic priests who devoted their lives to transforming Baja California's cultural landscape were scholars lettered in philosophy and the sciences, gentlemen attuned to contemporary Italian and Spanish baroque architecture and art. Many of them probably knew the buildings of Gian Lorenzo Bernini, perhaps even the paintings of Caravaggio and Diego Velázquez. The privileged priests reveled in the music of Johann Sebastian Bach and Antonio Vivaldi. They brought these sensitivities with them to the New World, where they came in contact with methods of construction and design practiced in the colonial cities of Nueva España. By later creating beautiful churches of their own while introducing visual art and music to Baja California's nomads, the padres brought baroque to the ends of the earth.

The singular emergence of the Jesuit Order injected fresh spiritual energy into Europe and set a vigorous course for New World colonization and enterprise. As one response of the Catholic Church to the Protestant Reformation, La Compañía de Jesús (the Society of Jesus) was recognized as a new religious order by Pope Paul III in 1540. Founded by Basque priest Ignatius of Loyola, the Society of Jesus became the spiritual and intellectual guiding light of Catholic Europe for the next two and one-half centuries. Through assignments abroad, the Jesuit mission was to spread Christianity, to send the Holy Spirit into the world, to propagate the faith in unconverted lands, to save souls.

Ignatius of Loyola (Iñigo de Oñaz y Loyola), a prominent Spanish knight who nearly perished at the Battle of Pamplona against the French in 1521, underwent spiritual conversion while recovering from his wounds. He abandoned his former life at court, temporarily becoming a hermit in search of solitude and incorporeal rebirth. He later studied for the priesthood in Spain and France. Living in Paris in 1534, he and six other priests committed themselves to serving the pope as missionaries. During the next years they formulated the aims of the Jesuit Order. These visionary priests, who broke bread together while discussing their ideas, named themselves La Compañía, from *comer pan*, meaning "to eat bread" in Spanish. The order developed into an efficient contemporary organization promoting self-examination, freedom of thought, honesty, and constructive discipline. Ignatius became the first father superior of the Society of Jesus. He was canonized by Pope Gregory XV in 1622 for emulating the lives of Jesus and Francis of Assisi.

The Society of Jesus was founded in part in reply to German theologian Martin Luther's posting of his "Ninety-Five Theses" on the Wittenberg Cathedral door in 1517. Luther's defiance sparked the Reformation, launching the Protestant movement throughout Europe. One answer of the Catholic Church to the Protestants was the Counter-Reformation, the Jesuit Order of Ignatius of Loyola seizing the torch to lead the Roman Catholic Church in a fresh direction. The Society of Jesus, a multinational force popular with young and vigorous European intellectuals, known for advances in philosophy and science, rose to dominate higher education circles of the Catholic world.

The Jesuits established a cohesive worldwide network that attracted people of prominence and wealth. Jesuit morality was believed superior to the two leading contemporary Catholic orders, the Franciscans and the Dominicans, both founded in the early thirteenth century. (The Franciscan Order was founded by the Italian friar Francis of Assisi [Saint Francis] in 1210, the Dominican Order in France by the Spanish friar Dominic of Osma [Saint Dominic] in 1217.) Jesuit ascendancy brought power to the organization and influence in all walks of life as well as political favors, financial contributions, and incredible freedoms. The Habsburg rulers of Spain favored the Jesuits because they were readily available, volunteered for the most daunting challenges, and delivered on their promises, earning the distrust and envy of their religious competitors. This favoritism of the Jesuits began to wane when the Bourbon rulers of Spain came to power in 1700. Aggressive Bourbon policies to control finance throughout the Spanish Empire caused them to closely observe and regulate far-reaching Jesuit business operations.

Hernán Cortés and the Discovery of Baja California

After the conquest of Tenochtitlan and the destruction of the Aztec Empire in 1521, the same year of Ignatius of Loyola's spiritual conversion, Spanish conquistador Hernán Cortés forged with his sword the new domain of Nueva España. Cortés began his rule in the name of the king of Spain, Charles I, also known as Charles V, Holy Roman emperor. Cortés demolished the temples of Tenochtitlan, erecting in their place a new capital, the Ciudad de México, Mexico City. Officially appointed governor-general by the Crown, Cortés founded Spanish colonial cities while promoting territorial expansion and evangelization. He developed agriculture and prospected for silver mines. Cortés incorporated the indigenous people into the realm by exploiting them as laborers.

While ruling the newly created Nueva España, Cortés promoted maritime conquest with the intention of expanding international sea trade. It was Cortés's persistence in sending out sea explorations that led to the discovery of Baja California. At first, from the Atlantic Ocean side of the New World (the Indies), Cortés sought entry to the Mar del Sur, or Southern Sea (the Pacific Ocean discovered by Vasco Núñez de Balboa in 1513), via a strait he thought existed across either the Isthmus of Tehuantepec or the Gulf of Honduras. Cortés hoped the discovery of a strait would lead quickly beyond the Indies to open sea, realizing a common but mistaken European belief that nearby, across this narrow sea, rested the continent of Asia and the Spice Islands.

During the early sixteenth century, conquistadores in the New World were bent on exploring Central and South America. These early explorers possessed no knowledge of the North American continent beyond Florida. They knew nothing about the Atlantic and Pacific coastlines of North America. They had no idea of the vastness of the Pacific Ocean. Cortés, in his fourth letter to the Spanish king (between 1519 and 1526 Cortés wrote five letters to Charles I describing his Mexican exploits—the *Cartas de relación*), mentioned his belief in a strait connecting the Atlantic Ocean to the Pacific Ocean. It may have been the popular early sixteenth-century novel by Garci Rodríguez de Montalvo, *Las sergas de Esplandián* (The Adventures of Esplandián), that gave credibility to geographical fantasies: "Know, that on the right hand of the Indies there is an island called California very close to the Terrestrial Paradise . . . and it is peopled by black women, without any men among them, for they live in the manner of Amazons." The inspiration for Montalvo naming the fictitious island California may have been his female character known as Calafia, who was an African monarch and a heroine of the adventures of Esplandián and other stories. Although Cortés does not mention this book or name California in his letters to Charles I, he may have heard about or even read the popular story.

Exhausted by his futile search to discover a new strait and, of course, with an eye out for the earthly paradise of Amazon women, Cortés and his soldiers trudged across the Isthmus of Tehuantepec to the Pacific Ocean side. In 1527 Cortés ordered the building of three ships in the port of Tehuantepec, Oaxaca, initiating the first of seven maritime explorations he sent out from the western seaboard of Mexico. Learning of Ferdinand Magellan's circumnavigation of the globe in 1522, Cortés organized a sea expedition, to be led by Álvaro de Saavedra, that would cross the Pacific Ocean to the Islas Filipinas, the Philippine Islands. Saavedra arrived in the Moluccas, the Spice Islands, with only one ship but failed to find a return Pacific route, dying in his attempt to reach Nueva España.

In 1528 Cortés returned to Spain to appear in person before Charles I, appealing for justice in answer to envious detractors who had decried his abuse of power in Nueva España and responding to their accusations that he withheld the *quinto real* (royal fifth), the Spanish Crown's taxation percentage on foreign enterprise. Cortés proved that he had delivered more than his share of taxes. He was decorated with the Order of Saint James and knighted marqués del Valle de Oaxaca (marquis of the Valley of Oaxaca). Returning to Mexico City in 1530, Cortés retained his position as military commander empowered for continued conquest, but he found himself demoted politically and in a power struggle with the newly appointed viceroy, Antonio de Mendoza.

The second sea expedition commissioned by Cortés, in 1532, captained by Diego Hurtado de Mendoza, discovered little more than a few islands off the coast of Nayarit. In October 1533 Cortés had two more caravels built in Tehuantepec, which disembarked to open sea from Manzanillo. Commanded by Fortún Jiménez, the mariners of this expedition discovered the Revillagigedo Islands out in the Pacific. After returning to Acapulco for refitting, Jiménez and his crew then continued in a more northwesterly direction, encountering new territory and thus becoming the first Spaniards to actually land on Baja California. While exploring inland, Fortún Jiménez was killed in an attack by the Pericú. The survivors of his expedition escaped back across the sea to Sinaloa. A fourth sea journey, under Fernando de Grijalva in 1534, headed even farther north to discover the body of water known today as the Gulf of California.

In April 1535 a fifth expedition, three hundred men under the command of Cortés himself, departed from Acapulco in three vessels with the intent of colonizing the newly discovered land. During the sea crossing, apparently impressed by frequent bright red sunsets across the water, Cortés named the expanse the Mar Bermejo, or Vermilion Sea. Cortés's party waded ashore in La Paz Bay. In his 1789 *Historia de la antigua o Baja California* (History of the ancient or Baja California), Jesuit historian Francisco Javier Clavijero opined that it may have been Cortés's description of Baja's climate and of a dramatic rock formation that caused the new territory to be named California. According to Clavijero, Cortés, suffering from the intense heat of La Paz, referred to the location as a *cálida fornax* (hot furnace), combining a Spanish word with a Latin word. Sailing out of La Paz Bay, the flotilla turned south around the cape to land near San Lucas. Cortés noted the natural stone arch at land's end and again used Spanish and Latin, calling the famous landmark *cala fornix* (arched cove). The heat and waterless wastes Cortés's party encountered discouraged explorations, as did the inhospitable bands of Guaycura and Pericú Indians. A frustrated Cortés returned to Nueva España without establishing a colony on Baja California.

After a sixth sea passage in 1537 ended in a second failed attempt to generate a Spanish colony in Baja's cape region, Cortés commissioned the final marine voyage of his tenure, that of Francisco de Ulloa, during 1539 and 1540. Cortés ordered Ulloa to explore the unknown sea believed to lie north of Mar Bermejo. In 1539 three caravels commanded by Ulloa embarked upon a journey into uncharted gulf waters. Two ships were lost early on, but, undaunted, Ulloa proceeded in the remaining vessel up the Sonora coast to discover the mouth of the Colorado River, not the expected sea passage to the Pacific. Ulloa tacked southward down the length of the Baja California land mass, westward around Cabo San Lucas, then into the Pacific Ocean, sailing north along the west Baja coastline as far as Isla Cedros, Island of Cedars. Ulloa became the first explorer to discover that Baja California was actually a peninsula. For some unknown reason, European cartographers continued to map Baja California as an island for another two centuries. Ulloa was also credited with naming the sea in Cortés's honor—Mar de Cortés, Sea of Cortés—the name for the gulf most commonly used in Mexico today. Tragically, Ulloa was murdered by one of his crew on the journey home.

Early Attempts to Colonize Baja California

Cortés returned to Spain in 1541. He died a rich man six years later, bitter at being ignored by the Spanish Crown. Nueva España was now completely controlled by Viceroy Antonio de Mendoza. Mendoza ordered his own sea expedition, undertaken during 1542 and 1543. Led by the Portuguese navigator Juan Rodríguez Cabrillo, this voyage departed for Baja California from Barra de Navidad on the coast of Jalisco. Cabrillo's instructions were to explore farther northward along the California coast. Three ships sailed up the west coast of the peninsula, going beyond Isla Cedros into uncharted territory past Ensenada, continuing on to San Diego Bay, passing Santa Catalina Island and today's Los Angeles, sailing onward to the north, and missing the entrance to San Francisco Bay (probably due to heavy fog, which often obscures it). Cabrillo's expedition reached the vicinity of Mendocino before turning back home with new and valuable information about Baja California and the northern coast.

During the second half of the sixteenth century, there were no major attempts to colonize Baja California. However, in 1564 five caravels and five hundred soldiers under the command of Miguel López de Legazpi were launched from Barra de Navidad. The flotilla crossed the Pacific Ocean to the Philippine Islands, now under Spanish control. In 1565 one of Legazpi's captains, Andrés de Urdaneta, by sailing far north of the Philippines, discovered trade winds and currents that returned his ship across the Pacific, bringing him to land near Mendocino, no longer terra incognita. Urdaneta continued south down the California coast to Cabo San Lucas and then sailed home to Acapulco.

Andrés de Urdaneta's revolutionary discovery of a trade wind sea route back to the New World from the

Orient initiated in 1568 Pacific Ocean crossings of Spanish treasure ships known as the Acapulco–Manila galleons. The annual trading journeys of these ships persisted for more than two centuries. These multisailed wooden cargo galleons, weighing up to 2,000 tons in their heyday, departed from Acapulco loaded with silver from the mines of Zacatecas destined for Manila in the Philippines. After the north Pacific crossing, galleons returned home to Nueva España by way of Baja California, carrying spices, silks, and other exotic luxury goods.

Spanish authorities realized the critical need to establish a secure port of call for these galleons in Baja California, the southern bays of Cabo San Lucas and San José del Cabo being prime candidates. Because of Baja California's lack of freshwater and food resources and menacing Pericú, Spanish colonists were unable to establish a permanent harbor colony until the mid-eighteenth-century at San José del Cabo, where galleon crews and passengers could find safe haven to rest and reprovision. Galleon crossings of the Pacific Ocean caused Spanish merchants, who had no way to protect the enormous commercial interests they had invested in these vulnerable ships, considerable worry due to piracy.

The worst of Spanish nightmares materialized when Francis Drake appeared off the Mexican coast in 1579. The English privateer had navigated the Atlantic Ocean, sailing south past Brazil, west through the Strait of Magellan, and then up the coast of South America and Mexico, ravaging port cities along the way. Drake crossed the Sea of Cortés to Baja California and sailed north along the California coast, eventually traversing the Pacific to circumnavigate the globe and returning home loaded with booty. In 1587 another English corsair, Thomas Cavendish, commanded three ships that crossed the Atlantic, menaced the coast of Brazil, and passed through the Strait of Magellan. Cavendish sacked South American ports and the coastal towns of Nueva España on his way north. He captured the gold-and-silver-laden 600-ton *Santa Ana* off Baja California's Cabo San Lucas, which he looted and burned. Cavendish successfully navigated the Pacific Ocean and made it back to England with his booty.

The viceroy of Nueva España finally responded to pirate incursions by sending Sebastián Vizcaíno in 1596 with three ships and a large number of soldiers to defend the Baja shipping lanes. Before making it to the lower cape, Vizcaíno sailed first to La Paz Bay, where he deposited forty men to try their luck at establishing a colony. After searching three months unsuccessfully for pirates along the coast of the southern peninsula, Vizcaíno returned to assess the progress of his La Paz colonists, rescuing them from starvation. The only attractive enterprise Baja California offered, it seemed, was diving for pearls, a seasonal activity. In 1599 Philip III, king of Spain, issued a *cédula real* (royal decree) to expel all pirates from Baja California, a command that was impossible to carry out.

In May 1602 Vizcaíno led a second voyage—this trip launched for the purpose of exploration—with four caravels and two hundred men, including the cartographer Jerónimo Martín Palacios and three Carmelite priests. The fleet reconnoitered the bays at San José del Cabo and Cabo San Lucas, then at Todos Santos on the Pacific side. Following the route of Juan Rodríguez Cabrillo sixty years earlier, Vizcaíno's expedition touched land at Ensenada and San Diego, continuing northward to Mendocino, also missing San Francisco Bay. The expedition returned to Acapulco in January 1603. During the next thirty years no further sea crossings were made to Baja California. Three new attempts to found colonies at La Paz Bay—two separate landings by Diego de Nava and by Esteban Carbonel during the 1630s, another in 1642 under Luis Cestín de Cañas—failed as before. Cañas, finding the natives docile, delivered word of familiar results to his superiors: colonization had proved impossible because of sterile land and lack of fresh water and food.

In 1643, in order to persuade the viceroy of Nueva España to continue the conquest of Baja California, the king of Spain, Philip IV, sent admiral Pedro Portel de Casanante across the Atlantic to form an expeditionary armada. He was ordered to conquer and populate California and to Christianize the barbarous natives. Preparations for this conquest of Baja California dragged on until 1648. During the expedition, Casanante explored the Sea of Cortés coast of the peninsula, abandoning the Baja California undertaking as too barren a land for conquest. Although no results from colonization were forthcoming for the next forty years, the Spanish Crown remained determined to seed Baja California with Spaniards for three strategic reasons: to protect and extend the frontiers of Nueva España; to provide a secure harbor for Acapulco–Manila galleon traffic; and to promote the spiritual conquest of the Catholic Church.

In September 1679, Charles II, king of Spain, issued a royal decree for the colonization of Baja California. The decree tendered substantial support to the governor of Sinaloa, Isidro Atondo y Antillón, including a military force, with a commission for priests of the Society of Jesus to accompany the expedition. The voyage to colonize Baja California was delayed until early 1683 due to the usual difficulties of distance and logistics. Ships of the Atondo expedition sailed from San Blas, Sinaloa, to La Paz in April 1683. Scouts quickly found a supply of fresh water, good fishing, and a fine place to erect a camp. The colonists began by building a chapel and small presidio. With the arrival of bands of Pericú and Guaycura, violence broke out between Indians and soldiers. The Jesuits, led by the Italian Eusebio Kino, including padres Copart, López, Goñí, and Quijosa, stepped in to defuse native anger with offers of food. Explorations of the Baja California interior caused subsequent Indian attacks. After a few months, plagued by dwindling water and food supplies, the colonizers returned to Sinaloa in order to recuperate. Departing La Paz, Atondo set off a mortar blast that left ten Guaycura stretched out dead on the beach.

In 1684 the revived Atondo expedition crossed the Sea of Cortés once again, relocating this time far north of La Paz along the central Baja California coast. Cochimí natives welcomed the landing party at a place the priests christened San Bruno. Atondo chose a site on an elevated mesa where the settlers began to build a presidio and a mission church, the first in California. At San Bruno the Spaniards thought they had found sufficient water and pasture for cattle. The Jesuits initiated Christian instruction to four hundred Cochimí. However, the colonization attempt of the second phase of the Atondo expedition also ended in failure for lack of water and food. The Spaniards, defeated by the elements, returned to Sinaloa in May 1685.

Establishing the Baja California Missions

Failure of the well-supported Atondo expedition made it difficult for the Jesuits to fund another effort to colonize Baja California. The persistent arguments of Padre Eusebio Kino and his new partner, Padre Juan María de Salvatierra, assisted by Jesuit benefactors in high places, gave the Jesuits another chance. The violence displayed by Atondo and his military contingent at La Paz bestowed upon Padre Kino an idea to conduct the conquest of California with a different twist. If the Jesuits funded their own mission, why couldn't they command their own soldiers? The padres established the basis for a theocracy.

In the name of Nuestra Señora de Loreto, on October 19, 1697, at the *entrada definitiva* (definitive entry), Padre Juan María de Salvatierra founded Loreto, the first permanent Spanish mission and town on Baja California. (Nuestra Señora de Loreto, Our Lady of Loreto, refers to the Virgin Mary and her pilgrimage site in Loreto, Italy, the final resting place of the Holy House where Mary was born, where the Annunciation took place, where Christ spent his childhood. This small house made of square red stones is said to have been miraculously transported from Nazareth to Italy by a band of angels in 1291.) The Monquí band of the Guaycura tribe called the place Conchó, probably meaning *aguaje* (waterhole). After crossing the Sea of Cortés from the mouth of the Yaqui River (a distance of 100 miles across the open sea) on the ship *Santa Elvira*, Salvatierra (*padre visitador* or *padre superior*, meaning superior of the Baja California Jesuit mission enterprise) and nine well-armed men waded ashore. Six days later, on October 25, a contingent of Monquí (a few of them San Bruno veterans) came to kiss the silver crucifix and wooden statue of the Virgin of Loreto that Salvatierra carried ashore.

Padre Kino, likewise a San Bruno veteran, originally disposed to accompany Padre Salvatierra, had remained in Sonora to deal with the revolt of 1695 in the Pimería Alta, the Spanish mission system of Sonora and southern Arizona. Kino, who always had Baja California on his mind, was replaced by another Italian Jesuit, Padre Francisco María Piccolo. Vocabularies recorded by French padre Juan Bautista Copart at San Bruno allowed Salvatierra to communicate with the Monquí and Cochimí. The location chosen to unload equipment and food stores, around which the pioneers set a temporary stockade of wooden stakes and cactus branches, was situated inland from the shoreline on a mile-wide alluvial plain, high ground between two arroyos covered with mesquite trees. Sheep, goats, pigs, cattle, and a horse were also brought to shore and into the stockade. The Spanish camp at the north arroyo overlooked the principal Monquí waterhole, a large stand of reeds, and the scattered encampment of Indian families beyond. Once the Spaniards were safely settled, Salvatierra gave thanks in an open-air service.

But then, on November 13, in an attempt to get hold of the Spaniards' food supply, some two hundred Monquí and Cochimí, hurling stones and shooting arrows, attacked the Spanish stronghold. The pioneers defended themselves with muskets and harquebus swivel guns. No Spaniards were seriously injured, but three Indians were killed, and many more were wounded. Two days after the Spanish victory, Salvatierra's party was reinforced by the launch *El Rosario*, which had been blown off course and separated from the *Santa Elvira* at their joint debarkation three weeks before. Five new men and supplies joined the settlers. The sloop sailed to Sonora's Yaqui River and then came back to Loreto one week later with Padre Piccolo. In the following months, the sixteen settlers erected a more substantial fortification, which became the first Real Presidio de Loreto, or Royal Fort of Loreto. With Indian help, the Spaniards went on to build corrals for the livestock and to begin clearing fields. They prepared the soil for planting, shoveled out irrigation ditches, and marked a permanent landing spot on the beach. Soon it became evident that the shortage of fresh water would severely limit the mission's success in producing crops.

The final battle for the domination of Loreto took place on Easter Sunday of 1698. Seeing their canoe had been stolen, ten armed Spanish soldiers marched up the coast to search for it. They found the canoe broken to pieces and encountered a group of warriors lying in ambush. Six natives were killed and several badly wounded in the ensuing skirmish. After the defeat the Monquí offered little armed resistance. With summer coming, another serious problem presented itself to the Baja California mission. Dependent on food supplied from Sonora, the starving men awaited the long-overdue delivery ship. The Monquí and Cochimí had already deserted the mission to harvest cactus fruits in the desert. At the last moment, the barque *San José* arrived to save the distressed Spanish settlers of Loreto from starvation, delivering foodstuffs and seven new volunteers, increasing the garrison to twenty-seven able-bodied men. To those willing to acknowledge it, the mission's fragility might have been a harbinger of things to come.

By October 1698 the first horseback exploration of Baja California under Padre Salvatierra ventured north, close to the abandoned San Bruno site, to the Cochimí ranchería and waterhole of Londó, where he and Padre Piccolo later established a *visita* (visiting station) for the Loreto mission, San Juan Bautista de Londó. Another expedition in May 1699, led by the energetic Piccolo, ascended the Sierra de la Giganta to the southwest through the watercourse known as Biaundó. They proceeded on to the Cochimí village of Viggé. Piccolo believed the wide, well-watered canyon offered a superior location for crops, orchards, and vineyards. Meanwhile, in Loreto, Salvatierra began construction of a proper mission church. Antonio García de Mendoza, the newly installed captain of the Loreto presidio, had completed a horse trail southwest to Viggé, a task that required clearing boulders from the 20-mile-long path. This trail initiated El Camino Real, the Royal Road, which would eventually traverse the peninsula to the south and then northward to connect all the future missions of Baja California.

Padre Piccolo, García de Mendoza, and a few garrison soldiers journeyed again to the Cochimí ranchería, this time to start the building of a mission and church. Indian laborers set stone foundations, made adobe bricks, and laid the walls for a chapel, priest quarters, and reception room. With Cochimí guides, Piccolo and García de Mendoza continued on beyond the mountains to the Pacific Ocean side of Baja. They searched the coast to locate a good harbor for the Manila galleon. Without success, the explorers returned to Viggé. Having finished the construction of the three mission buildings at Viggé on December 3, 1699, before the massed Indians, Padre Piccolo dedicated San Francisco Javier Viggé Biaundó, the second enduring mission of Baja California.

In early 1700 Padre Salvatierra mailed a petition to the viceroy of Nueva España, José Sarmiento Valladares, requesting funding for the Jesuit effort, listing the needs and hardships of the California missions. Salvatierra made it clear that the missions relied solely on private donations and could no longer survive without royal support. They couldn't meet soldier payroll and had lost their supply ship from Sonora. Salvatierra pointed out that the Jesuits gave plenty in return to the Spanish Crown: new lands, rich pearling beds in the south, the salvation of souls. Padre Salvatierra traveled to Mexico City to follow up his arguments in person and to enlist Padre Juan de Ugarte to his cause.

The death of childless Charles II in 1700 spelled the end of Spain's Habsburg dynasty. Philip, duke of Anjou, grandson of Louis XIV of France, was installed as Philip V, the new king of Spain. Bourbon administrators set about ordering the Habsburg financial disarray. They attempted to wrest power from the Spanish nobility, to redirect taxation and the flow of money into royal coffers. Waves made by the new regime were felt by Baja California missionaries. Jesuit expenditures acceptable in Habsburg terms did not sit well with pragmatic Bourbon financiers, who demanded economic development and expressed little concern for saving souls. In the spiritual realm, Franciscan and Dominican jealousy pressured the Jesuits, already under attack from Nueva España entrepreneurs who wanted Baja California opened to private development.

Feeling the squeeze to maintain a foothold on the peninsula after just two years, the Jesuits were afraid an independent soldiery would destroy their mission. They feared New Spain's frontier folk, the rabble of Sonora and Sinaloa, being let loose among their Indians. It wasn't enough for the Jesuits to explore and conquer Baja California, convert the natives, sow the fields, and build churches. They also had to satisfy the royal Spanish bureaucrats with discreet diplomacy. Fortunately, as the educators and confessors of Spanish royalty and the nobility, the Jesuits maintained their position of power.

Charismatic Honduran padre Juan de Ugarte arrived at Loreto in March 1701 to reinforce padres Salvatierra and Piccolo. In answer to Salvatierra's plea, a cédula real had been enacted to release six thousand pesos annually in support of the Baja California missions. Padre Piccolo traveled to Guadalajara and Mexico City to plead for more funding. The marqués de Villapuente answered Piccolo's prayers by promising endowments for three new missions. A decree was issued in 1703 to establish a presidio at Cabo San Lucas as a way station for the Manila galleon. Although this action was not carried out for another three decades, it put pressure on the Jesuits. Later that year three pearling ships capsized in a storm off Loreto, delivering eighty-four men into Jesuit hands, unwanted mouths to feed for the next two months until their crafts were repaired.

By 1705 land and sea expeditions north and south of Loreto under padres Ugarte and Piccolo led to the establishment of two new missions, Santa Rosalía de Mulegé and San Juan Bautista de Liguí. San José de Comondú was founded in the Sierra de la Giganta during 1708, funded by one of the Villapuente endowments. Padre Piccolo's central Baja California exploration of 1709 discovered the future mission sites of Nuestra Señora de Guadalupe Guasinapí and La Purísima Concepción de Cadegomó, founded a decade later along good watercourses of the western Sierra de la Giganta. The year 1709 marked the beginning of a devastating five-year drought and lethal smallpox epidemic in which 50 percent of central Baja California's mission converts died. As a result of these disasters, little progress was made until the rains returned in 1715.

Padre Salvatierra sailed in 1716 from Loreto to La Paz with the intent of establishing a coastal mission in Guaycura country, but this venture ended in failure. Piccolo undertook his last expedition inland and discovered the freshwater lake at Kadakaamán, the future site for San Ignacio Mission. In 1717 Padre Salvatierra and Padre Jaime Bravo set out for Mexico City to meet the new viceroy, Baltasar de Zuñiga y Guzmán. Salvatierra, revered leader of the Jesuit conquest of California, collapsed and died in Guadalajara.

Juan María de Salvatierra was temporarily succeeded as *padre visitador* by Padre Jaime Bravo, then permanently by Padre Juan de Ugarte in 1720. In 1719 Padre Ugarte tackled the chronic need for a dependable ship to transport food and livestock to Loreto from the productive missions of Sonora's Yaqui River valley. To solve the problem of leaky supply boats continually being lost at sea, Padre Ugarte decided to manufacture a sturdy ship with local wood. His task was to find a tall, straight tree from which to form support beams and planks. In the canyons of the Sierra de la Giganta above Mulegé, Ugarte and his men found stands of the guéribo tree, a 50- to 60-foot-high poplar. Ugarte's team of woodcutters and shipwrights cut timbers for the keel, framework, and hull of the boat. Oxcarts transported the wood to Mulegé, the whole exercise taking one year. The 50-foot-long boat, christened *El Triunfo de la Cruz*, gave Ugarte and the Loreto mission many years of reliable service. On its maiden voyage in May 1721, Padre Ugarte reconnoitered the upper gulf to encounter the Colorado River but found no passage to open ocean. Ugarte's journey confirmed the results of the Francisco de Ulloa expedition of 1538: Baja was indeed a peninsula.

Between 1719 and 1721 four new missions were created: Nuestra Señora de Guadalupe and La Purísima Concepción de Cadegomó in central Baja among the Cochimí, and Nuestra Señora de Dolores Apaté near the coast north of La Paz Bay and Nuestra Señora del Pilar Airapí at the La Paz colony, these two missions targeting the Guaycura and Pericú for congregation and conversion. Although some Jesuits preferred northward expansion from Loreto to work among the more amenable Cochimí, Padre Ugarte knew the importance of satisfying the two pressing concerns of Viceroy Zuñiga y Guzmán in Mexico City: to round up the bands of Guaycura and Pericú that still rampaged the cape in defiant freedom (the only thing these tribes had in common was their hatred of the priests and Spanish soldiers) and to establish a safe port for protection of Manila galleon traffic. Padre Ugarte did send another expedition, led by Padre Clemente Guillén, to Magdalena Bay on the Pacific coast in hope of locating a suitable anchorage for the galleons, but a deep, protected harbor was not to be found.

Due to the lack of fresh water, the area around La Paz was home to no particular Indian band, yet sooner or later most of the southern tribes came to harvest the bounty of La Paz's teeming bay. The natives were sometimes captured while fishing the bay, then brought to La Paz and the Nuestra Señora del Pilar mission. It remained a daunting task to pacify the antagonistic Guaycura and Pericú bands, reluctant neophytes who hated the Spaniards and never ceased fighting among themselves. Despite these chronic conflicts, Padre Ugarte remained committed to evangelizing southern Baja California. In 1721 Guaycura at the exhausted Liguí mission south of Loreto were relocated by Padre Guillén farther down the coast to Nuestra Señora de los Dolores Apaté, Liguí and Dolores Apaté being coastal missions soon destined for abandonment. In 1724 Italian padre Ignacio María Nápoli established Misión Santiago Apóstol Aiñiní on the eastern slopes of the Sierra de la Laguna, a location that proved suited for long-term success. Back in Cochimí territory to the north, Padre Juan Bautista María de Luyando founded Misión San Ignacio de Kadakaamán in 1728. With the spectacular success of Misión San Ignacio during its first decade, a new church was built a day's journey to the north, Misión San Pablo becoming San Ignacio's visiting station by 1740. Jesuits and neophytes mourned their beloved Padre Piccolo, who died at Loreto in 1729.

In 1730 Spanish padre Nicolás Tamaral founded San José del Cabo Añuití at the southern tip of the peninsula. On the Pacific coast side of the cape, Santa Rosa de las Palmas, with sufficient water, rich grazing, and tillable land, was established at Todos Santos by Italian Jesuit Sigismundo Taraval in 1733. Soon after being congregated to the new Santa Rosa mission, hundreds of Guaycura converts were wiped out by virulent smallpox and measles epidemics. Padre Taraval then brought in bands of Pericú to repopulate Santa Rosa de las Palmas and work the mission land. Epidemics continued to decimate these southern tribes during the ensuing years. In one generation an estimated original population of eight thousand Guaycura and Pericú was reduced by 50 percent. While the priests and soldiers of the south were corralling the last recalcitrant natives, another invisible killer, syphilis, was exacting a heavy toll on Indian women and their newborns.

The Manila galleon put into San José del Cabo in January 1734. *Nuestra Señora del Pilar de Zaragosa* became the first Spanish ship to find safe harbor since the Jesuits established four successful missions in the cape. Fed fresh meat and pitaya fruit, the exhausted galleon crew quickly rebounded from scurvy, while the seriously ill ship's captain, José Francisco de Baitos, and Augustinian padre Domingo de Horbigoso were nursed back to health by Padre Tamaral. These actions elicited a positive response from Nueva España's latest viceroy, Juan Antonio de Vizarrón, who quickly designated San José del Cabo port of call for all Manila galleon traffic. It appeared that padre visitador Juan de Ugarte's campaign to settle southern Baja California was finally working.

However, by the summer of 1734 traumatized neophytes of the four southern missions had erupted in rebellion against the harsh rule of the priests and Spanish soldiers. Fomented by deposed chiefs and shamans, the Guaycura were the first to revolt in what was to become an all-out insurrection against the poorly guarded churches of the region. Padre Tamaral, his assistant, Padre Lorenzo Carranco, and two neophyte servants were clubbed to death, their bodies mutilated at the San José del Cabo church. Pericú rebels killed a guard at Nuestra Señora del Pilar in La Paz and torched the mission of Santiago Apóstol Aiñiní. Padre Taraval, who fled at the last minute, barely escaped the burning of his mission, Santa Rosa de las Palmas at Todos Santos. For once, traditional Indian enemies had mobilized together to at least temporarily throw off the Jesuit yoke.

Soldiers from Sonora had arrived at the Nuestra Señora de los Dolores Apaté mission north of La Paz by early 1735. They attempted to hunt down Guaycura and Pericú rebels running loose across the cape, but with no results. In January 1735 the Manila galleon put in for the second time at San José del Cabo. Unaware of the native rebellion, thirteen sailors sent ashore in a longboat to greet the missionaries of San José del Cabo Añuití were ambushed and slain by Pericú warriors. The rebels attacked the unsuspecting galleon as it lay anchored in the harbor. Fortunately, the ship and its crew escaped, sailing on to Acapulco. The natives destroyed all four southern missions and murdered a host of Spaniards. The Manila galleon had lost its newfound port. Viceroy Vizarrón was accused by the Jesuits of dereliction of duty. He had not answered their pleas to provide soldiers to defend the missions. To deal with the rebellion, Vizarrón enlisted Manuel Bernal de Huidobro, the militant governor of Sinaloa. Huidobro, like his superior, distrusted the Jesuits. In agreement with Vizarrón, Huidobro wanted Baja California's Jesuit-controlled land and its neophyte labor released to private development by Spanish gente de razón.

Huidobro departed overland from Loreto for La Paz in February 1736 with forty soldiers, ostensibly to reconquer the south. Upon arrival he took sides with the Indian chiefs, a move intended to show the Jesuits that he was in control. This unexpected attitude infuriated the padres. Huidobro eventually rounded up Guaycura and Pericú leaders, exiling them to mainland Nueva España. The rebels finally sued for peace. While Huidobro installed permanent military detachments at La Paz, San José del Cabo, and Todos Santos, the Jesuits shifted their focus north of the cape. The German padre Lamberto Hostell established a new mission in northern Guaycura territory at San Luis Gonzaga Chiriyaqui in 1737, later founding, by the coast of the southern Sierra de la Giganta, Misión La Pasión (Nuestra Señora de los Dolores Chillá), which replaced Dolores de Apaté to its north as the visita of San Luis Gonzaga. At that time, Guaycura and Pericú, who survived the epidemics, were transferred to San Luis Gonzaga, La Pasión, and missions in Cochimí territory. It became evident that Jesuit power was melting away in the peninsular south. The Jesuits no longer controlled the military. They were made to relinquish vast tracts of land, tilling only small plots attached to their churches. While diseases killed the Indians, colonists from Nueva España flocked to the newly opened southern Baja California territories to try their luck at farming, ranching, and mining.

In the Sierra de la Giganta of central Baja California, in contrast to what was happening with the rapid decline of Guaycura and Pericú populations in the cape, the Cochimí were reproducing, their numbers on the rebound. The Jesuit mission achievement reached its high point between 1740 and 1760. Sixty years after the definitive entry at Loreto, as a result of tremendous sacrifice and hardship, the Jesuits had transformed third-generation Cochimí neophytes into Roman Catholics, actually creating a new society based on rural farming and animal husbandry. At their most successful missions, the Jesuits moved beyond the first rustic adobe churches to erect in their place three of Baja California's four great baroque stone churches: the beautiful temple of Nuestra Señora de Loreto Conchó; the architectural wonder at San Francisco Javier Viggé Biaundó; and the largest, most elaborate temple on California soil, San José de Comondú. The fourth great baroque stone church, yet to be built, was San Ignacio de Kadakaamán. During this productive period, the Jesuits renewed their efforts to attract endowments, advancing to establish missions among the northern Cochimí. In 1751, with the congregation of hundreds of neophytes, Padre Jorge Retz founded Misión Santa Gertrudis de Cadacamán. The Jesuit Wenceslao Linck established another thriving mission among the Cochimí in 1762 north of Santa Gertrudis, Misión San Francisco de Borja Adac. The last Jesuit mission, Santa María de los Angeles Cabujakaamung, its adobe ruins located east of Cataviña, was founded in 1767 and then abandoned two years later.

At the height of the Jesuit achievement in Baja California, the years 1767 and 1768 brought unforeseen changes of momentous consequence to the missions. After more than two centuries of receiving high favor from the Catholic kings of Europe, in 1767, by royal decree, the Jesuits were expelled without trial from Baja California, from Nueva España, from all their missions worldwide. As a result of secret meetings, autocratic Catholic rulers and their ministers, led by Charles III of Spain, responding to a list of never-proven allegations, ousted the Society of Jesus from its territories. It was not a judicial sentence but a total Bourbon economic takeover, a coordinated seizure of Jesuit holdings, of their churches, properties, and revenues. Stripped of power and possessions, Jesuits in Catholic countries were arrested like convicts and deported to the island of Corsica. The isolated Jesuits of Baja California were removed in 1768, herded to Mexico City, then shipped to Europe. The kingdoms of Prussia, Poland, and Russia did not heed the Bourbon decree, so Jesuits survived in those countries. The Jesuit Order was finally reinstated by Pope Pius VII in 1814.

The removal of sixteen Jesuit priests was a devastating blow to mission Indians, especially to the Cochimí of central Baja. They lost their mentors and protectors in civilization. It was the same fate for other settled Indians in the north and other parts of mainland Nueva España. People of mixed race and the poor were also disenfranchised. To xenophobic Hispanics of Nueva España, resentful of Jesuit economic power, the expulsion of these foreigners who had consistently outmaneuvered their own civil and military officials was a deliverance. Entrepreneurs were at last free to develop the land and exploit Indian labor. New colonists brought new waves of disease to Baja California.

Padre Junípero Serra, the Spanish Franciscan and new padre superior who had already established five missions in Querétaro's Sierra Gorda of central Nueva España, arrived at Loreto in April 1768. He brought fifteen priests of the Franciscan Order to replace the expelled Jesuits. They stayed in Baja California for only five years, from 1768 to 1772. During this time, Padre Serra founded a mission among the Cochimí, San Fernando Rey de Velicatá, while Padre Francisco Palou built the church of La Presentación as a visita to San Javier Mission. Inspector General José de Gálvez, who had overseen the Jesuit deportation from Baja California, returned to inspect the missions under the Franciscan Order. He discovered abuses of the *comisarios*, the gente de razón supply managers, now acting independently of the priests, who were squandering mission property and mistreating the Indians. Gálvez returned the power of supply distribution to the Franciscan priests, de facto powers that were once held by the Jesuits.

In 1772, coveting participation in the Baja California adventure, the Dominican Order, whose principal field of colonial operation was in Oaxaca, led by padre superior Juan Pedro de Iriarte, struck a deal with the Franciscans to cede the Baja California peninsula to the Dominicans. Baja's Franciscan priests followed the departed Padre Serra to greener pastures of Alta, or Upper, California. The Spanish plan of northward territorial expansion was bent on establishing presidios and missions from San Diego on the coastline north to Monterey, in part to counter landings by British and Russian mariners. Padre Serra and his successors founded twenty-one Spanish Franciscan missions in Alta California from 1769 to 1823, extending El Camino Real to San Francisco. In 1848, as a result of the Mexican-American War and the Treaty of Guadalupe Hidalgo, Alta California was ceded to the United States of America, along with most of Arizona, New Mexico, and Texas.

To take control of Baja California, the first Dominican priests came ashore at Loreto in October 1772 to await the arrival of their leader, padre superior Iriarte. One month later Padre Iriarte was shipwrecked and drowned while crossing the Sea of Cortés. Padre Vicente de Mora, elected the new leader, took over Dominican operations in Loreto. Padre Mora assigned his host of priests to occupy the already established Baja California missions. A few years later, in 1776, indicating the Spanish Crown's shift of territorial interest, the Dominicans in Loreto lost their station as head of the California missions to Monterey and the Franciscans. Throughout the course of their sixty-eight-year occupation of Baja California (from 1772 to 1840), in order to fill the gap north to Franciscan territory in Alta California, Dominicans established nine missions in the northern quarter of the peninsula, a region they called La Frontera, the frontier. Unlike the international mix of Jesuit priests who had been expelled, Dominican missionaries in Baja California were primarily criollos, men of European descent born in Nueva España.

In 1774 Padre Mora founded Baja California's first Dominican mission, Nuestra Señora del Rosario de Viñadaco, the northernmost and last outpost among the Cochimí. A second church was built a few miles down the arroyo after the well of the first church ran dry. As they scouted northward into unknown territory, the priests encountered tribes unrelated to the Cochimí of central Baja California. These were Yuman, including the Kiliwa, Pai Pai, and Cucupá, people who lived in rancherías of the Sierra San Pedro Mártir, along the Pacific coast, and east across the peninsula to the Colorado River. The Yuman enjoyed a milder, moister climate in the north, harvesting more abundant food resources: piñon nuts, agave hearts, mesquite beans, cactus fruits, wild honey, deer, mountain sheep, jackrabbits, abalone, crabs, and shellfish. A few Yuman even entered the international market by selling sea otter skins to whalers and pirates. Neighboring bands of Yuman spoke dialects unintelligible to each other. Like the other peninsular tribes, the Cochimí, Guaycura, and Pericú, the Yuman fought among themselves, failing to unite against the dictator priests and Spanish military. Population estimates of the Yuman living in Baja California's northern quarter during the 1770s vary from five to ten thousand people. With devastating smallpox epidemics racing through the north in 1777, 1781, and 1794, Yuman numbers plummeted by more than 95 percent during the next generation until final abandonment of the northern missions by 1840.

In order to establish their missions, Dominican priests, like the Jesuits and Franciscans before them, searched for freshwater springs, arable land, good pasture, and trees to provide firewood. With soldiers leading the way, they rounded up the Yuman. They brought bands of them to the missions for baptism and conversion, to work the fields, and to tend the flocks. To the Spanish Crown, the value of the northern peninsular Dominican missions and military presidios was to facilitate land communications between Sonora and Alta California, to protect the territory from foreign encroachment by sea.

The final eight Dominican missions created on Baja California ministering the Yuman tribes were Santo Domingo de la Frontera in 1775, founded by padres Manuel García and Miguel Hidalgo; San Vicente Ferrer in 1780, their largest and most successful mission, established by padres Miguel Hidalgo and Joaquín Valero; San Miguel Arcángel de la Frontera in 1787, founded by Padre Luis de Sales; Santo Tomás de Aquino in 1791, established by padres José Loriente and Juan Crisóstomo Gómez, Padre Gómez coming north after completing the church at San Ignacio; San Pedro Mártir de Verona in 1794, founded by padres Cayetano Paya, José Loriente, Juan Pablo Grijalva, and Juan Crisóstomo Gómez; Santa Catalina Virgen y Mártir in 1797, established by padres José Loriente and Tomás Valdellón; El Descanso in 1812, founded by Padre Tomás Ahumada; and Nuestra Señora de Guadalupe del Norte in 1834, established by Padre Félix Caballero.

As disease-ravaged Yuman Indians of the Dominican missions in northern Baja California hovered near extinction, earth-shaking changes were occurring in the heart of Nueva España. After widespread rebellion against the Spanish, the War of Mexican Independence became a reality in 1810, Mexico finally gaining its freedom from Spain in 1821. By 1834 the Mexican government had secularized all the missions. The last of the Dominicans departed Baja California in 1840. The deserted mission churches built by the Dominicans in Yuman territory were all erected of sun-dried adobes; consequently, these temples exist today as little more than broken-down walls. Three exceptional Dominican churches do survive on the peninsula, ones finished in stone at sites pioneered among the Cochimí by the Jesuits: San Ignacio de Kadakaamán, completed in 1786; Santa Gertrudis de Cadacamán, finished in 1796; and San Francisco de Borja Adac, completed in 1801.

Baja California Missions Time Line

*** original stone churches
** rebuilt modern churches
* churches/foundations in ruins
(see Baja California map)

J Jesuit
F Franciscan
D Dominican

1. San Bruno: founded in 1684 by Eusebio Kino (J); abandoned in 1685*
2. Nuestra Señora de Loreto Conchó: founded in 1697 by Juan María de Salvatierra (**J**); abandoned in 1829; church completed in 1744 by Jaime Bravo (**J**)***
3. Visita San Juan Bautista Londó: founded in 1699 by Juan María de Salvatierra and Francisco María Piccolo (**J**); abandoned in 1750*
4. San Francisco Javier Viggé Biaundó: founded in 1699 by Francisco María Piccolo (**J**); abandoned in 1817; church completed in 1758 by Miguel del Barco (**J**)***
5. San Juan Bautista Liguí: founded in 1705 by Pedro de Ugarte (**J**); abandoned in 1721*
6. Santa Rosalía de Mulegé: founded in 1705 by Juan Manuel de Basaldúa (**J**); abandoned in 1828; church completed in 1766 by Francisco Escalante (**J**)***
7. San José de Comondú: founded in 1736 by Julián de Mayorga (**J**); abandoned in 1827; church completed in 1762 by Francisco Inama (**J**) at the 1737 site of Francisco Wagner (**J**)***
8. San Miguel de Comondú: founded in 1736 by Julián de Mayorga; abandoned in 1737*
9. La Purísima Concepción de Cadegomó: founded in 1720 by Nicolás Tamaral (**J**); abandoned in 1822*
10. Nuestra Señora del Pilar Airapí: founded in 1720 by Jaime Bravo and Juan de Ugarte (**J**); abandoned in 1748**
11. Nuestra Señora de Guadalupe Guasinapí: founded in 1720 by Everardo Helen (**J**); abandoned in 1795*
12. Nuestra Señora de los Dolores Apaté: founded in 1721 by Clemente Guillén (**J**); abandoned in 1741*
13. Santiago Apóstol Aiñiní: founded in 1724 by Ignacio María Nápoli (**J**); abandoned in 1795**
14. San Ignacio de Kadakaamán: founded in 1728 by Juan Bautista de Luyando (**J**); abandoned in 1840; church completed in 1786 by Juan Crisóstomo Gómez (**D**)***
15. San José del Cabo Añuití: founded in 1730 by Nicolás Tamaral (**J**); abandoned in 1840**
16. Santa Rosa de las Palmas: founded in 1733 by Sigismundo Taraval (**J**); abandoned in 1825**
17. San Luis Gonzaga Chiriyaqui: founded in 1737 by Lamberto Hostell (**J**); abandoned in 1768; church completed in 1758 by Juan Jacobo Baegert (**J**)***
18. Visita San Pablo: founded in 1740 by Fernando Consag (**J**); abandoned in 1780*
19. La Pasión (Dolores Chillá): founded in 1741 by Lamberto Hostell (**J**); abandoned in 1768*
20. Santa Gertrudis de Cadacamán: founded in 1751 by Jorge Retz (**J**); abandoned in 1822; church completed in 1796 by Dominicans***
21. San Francisco de Borja Adac: founded in 1762 by Wenceslao Linck (**J**); abandoned in 1818; church completed in 1801 by Dominicans***
22. Santa María de los Angeles Cabujakaamung: founded in 1767 by Victoriano Arnés (**J**); abandoned in 1769*
23. San Fernando Rey de Velicatá: founded in 1769 by Junípero Serra (**F**); abandoned in 1818*
24. Visita La Presentación: founded in 1769 by Francisco Palou (**F**); abandoned in 1817*
25. Nuestra Señora del Rosario Viñadaco (1): founded in 1774 by Vicente Mora (**D**); abandoned in 1776*
26. Nuestra Señora del Rosario Viñadaco (2): founded in 1776 by Francisco Galisteo (**D**); abandoned in 1832*
27. Santo Domingo de la Frontera: founded in 1775 by Manuel García and Miguel Hidalgo (**D**); abandoned in 1839*
28. San Vicente Ferrer: founded in 1780 by Miguel Hidalgo and Joaquín Valero (**D**); abandoned in 1833*
29. San Miguel Arcángel: founded in 1787 by Luis de Sales (**D**); abandoned in 1833*
30. Santo Tomás de Aquino: founded in 1791 by José Loriente (**D**); abandoned in 1840*
31. San Pedro Mártir de Verona: founded in 1794 by José Loriente (**D**); abandoned in 1824*
32. Santa Catalina Virgen y Mártir: founded in 1797 by José Loriente (**D**); abandoned in 1840*
33. El Descanso: founded in 1817 by Tomás de Ahumada (**D**); abandoned in 1834**
34. Nuestra Señora de Guadalupe: founded in 1834 by Félix Caballero (**D**); abandoned in 1840*

The Intact Eighteenth-Century Churches of Baja California

1.1. Restored Loreto church: façade, main entry, east courtyard archway. The bell tower was added in the 1950s.

Misión Nuestra Señora de Loreto Conchó, 1697

The mission church of Nuestra Señora de Loreto Conchó stands solid and tall in the heart of Loreto, Baja California Sur, a lovely coastal town on the Sea of Cortés located approximately at midpeninsula. The definitive establishment of Loreto mission, the first successful European settlement on Baja California, served as the Jesuit base for colonization of the peninsula. Nuestra Señora de Loreto Conchó was founded in 1697 by the Italian padre Juan María de Salvatierra. The Loreto church functioned until 1776 as head of the Baja and Alta California missions. The mission was officially abandoned in 1822, but the outpost town of Loreto and its mission church struggled on, surviving until the present day. The annual Loreto mission festival runs from October 19 to 25.

Loreto is connected to the rest of Baja California by the Transpeninsular Highway, Mexico Highway #1. After crossing the US border into Mexico through either Tijuana, Tecate, or Mexicali, connecting south via the Pacific coast city of Ensenada, it's a tortuous eighteen-hour, 400-mile drive south to Loreto. The dangerous two-lane paved highway, shoulderless and narrow, winds through spectacular mountain and desert vistas. Driving north from Cabo San Lucas, located at the southern tip of Baja California, it takes two hours (80 miles) to get to La Paz via Mexico Highway #19, then another five hours (200 miles) more before reaching Loreto on Mexico Highway #1. A car ferry crosses the Sea of Cortés several times a week from Guaymas, Sonora, to Santa Rosalía (125 miles north of Loreto) and from Topolobampo, Sinaloa, to La Paz. Daily airline flights arrive in Loreto from Los Angeles and several Mexican cities.

Loreto, today's thriving sun and sea tourist destination with a population of twelve thousand, lies at the base of the Sierra de la Giganta, an impressive backdrop of jagged volcanic mountains rising to the west and paralleling the coast. Peaks of the Sierra de la Giganta reach over 5,000 feet in elevation. Offshore from Loreto, angled to the southwest, stretches the 30-mile-long Isla del Carmen. Loreto's shaded central business and residential district nestles around the enduring Misión Nuestra Señora de Loreto Conchó church, the town's principal landmark.

Entering Loreto off Mexico Highway #1, the main thoroughfare, Avenida Salvatierra, leads directly to the town center. Three blocks before reaching the church, the street jogs south, routing into Avenida Hidalgo. At that point, Avenida Salvatierra continues as a pedestrian mall, passing in front of the church and the connected historical museum. The attractive pedestrian walkway and Avenida Hidalgo pass through the central district of hotels, restaurants, gift shops, and the civic plaza. Loreto's vanished presidio once stood near this square. A long block beyond the plaza, the two central avenues reach Calle de la Playa, a handsome street lined with palms and luxury hotels that face out to sea across the *malecón* (jetty). A lovely beach drive and promenade lead north to the marina.

The precisely cut cream-colored stone walls of the Nuestra Señora de Loreto mission church (figures 1.1, 1.2), restored in the early twentieth century, incorporate some of the original facing masonry (over a rubble interior) of Mexican padre Jaime Bravo's church, which was completed in 1744. Bravo's church was heavily damaged during the earthquake of 1877, which caused the collapse of the original bell tower. The main altar screen and interior decorations, more recently restored, were first installed in the 1750s. Padre Bravo's church rests on the site of the original sun-dried adobe-brick structure begun by Padre Salvatierra in 1699 and finished in 1704. The main entrance to the Loreto church (figure 1.5) is oriented to the southeast at 140 degrees. Above the entry stands a recent stone statue of Our Lady of Loreto and Child (figure 1.4), with an older inscription below proclaiming Loreto as head of the Baja and Alta

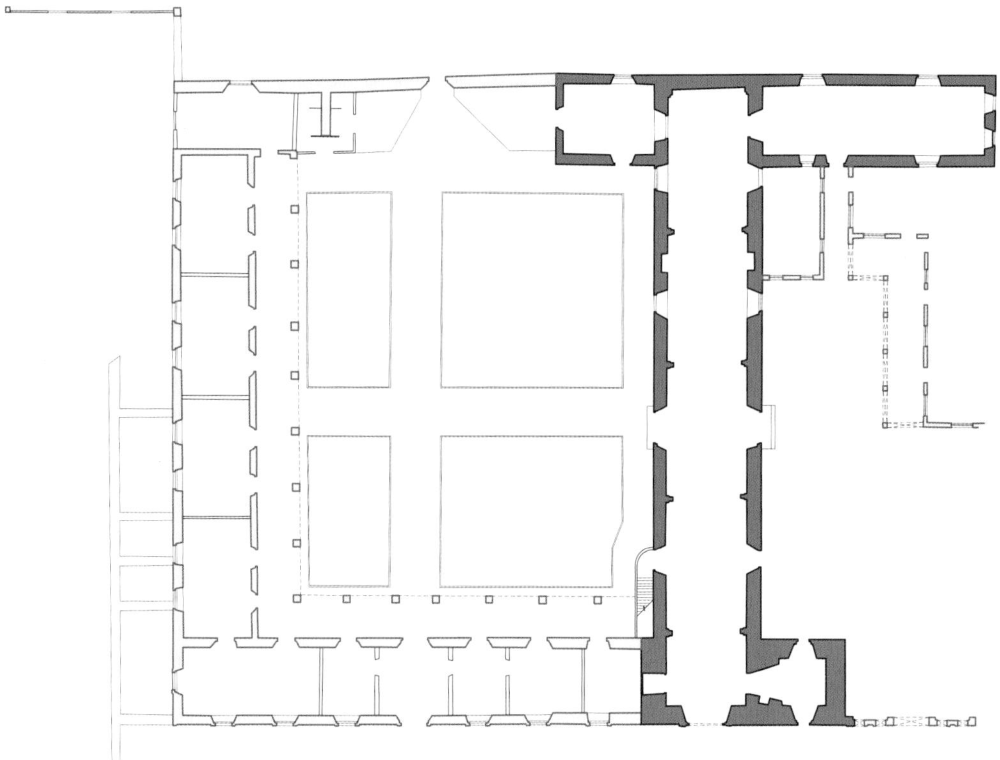

Misión Nuestra Señora de Loreto Conchó

California missions. The restored church, laid out in rectangular form with two side entryways, spans 150 feet in length and 20 feet in width. A 30-foot-high flat ceiling spreads across a length of cedar-wood beams as it proceeds from the entryway (figure 1.6) down the arched and pillared nave to the main altar (figure 1.7).

A photograph taken on the church's rooftop in 1905 shows three bronze bells hung by ropes from an elevated tree trunk. During the quake of 1938, the ceiling caved in, causing considerable damage. Today's church reveals a lofty campanile (figure 1.1), unfortunately completely out of proportion with the rest of the building. This bell tower, about 75 feet high and completed in 1955, was commissioned by Padre Modesto Sánchez Moyón with funds gained from winning the Mexican National Lottery. During the 1950s, Padre Sánchez made contributions to the church's restoration, to Loreto's schools, and to other civic projects. A museum guard offered another story of how the tower was funded, suggesting the priest discovered a treasure under one of the church walls.

American author John Steinbeck visited Loreto's church in 1940. In his book *The Log from the Sea of Cortez*, Steinbeck wrote:

> The roof had fallen in and the main body of the church was a mass of rubble. From the walls hung the shreds of old paintings. . . . One small chapel was intact in the church, but the door to it was barred by a wooden grille, and we had to peer through into the small, dark, cool room. There were paintings on the walls, one of which we wanted badly to see more closely, for it looked very much like

> an El Greco, and probably was not painted by El Greco. . . . The Virgin Herself, Our Lady of Loreto, was in a glass case and surrounded by the lilies of the recently past Easter. In the dim light of the chapel she seemed very lovely. (143, 144)

Steinbeck speculated about the Jesuits and the environment:

> It must have been a difficult task for those first sturdy Jesuit fathers to impress the Indians of the Gulf. The air here is very miraculous, and outlines of reality change with the moment. The sky sucks up the land and disgorges it. A dream hangs over the whole region, a brooding kind of hallucination. Perhaps only the shock of a seventeenth century wood-carving (Our Lady of Loreto) could do the trick: surely the miracle must have been virile to be effective. (68)

Stepping into the restored church with its steep, pure white walls, the feeling is cool, light, and airy. Two entryway side chapels with grilled wooden doors face each other. The choir loft hangs above these side chapels (figure 1.14). The rear wall of the east side chapel contains a wooden sculpture (figure 1.12) of the crucified Christ, flanked on both sides by statues of Nuestra Señora de los Dolores (Our Lady of Sorrows) and San Antonio holding baby Jesús. In the west side chapel stands a life-sized sculpture of a bloody, scourged Christ (figure 1.13). Checkered floor tiles lead between the pews to the main altar. Actually, two Our Lady of Loreto statues can be found inside the church. The most noticeable image of Nuestra Señora de Loreto stands within the glass-encased central niche of the restored main altar, or *retablo* (altarpiece of niches) (figure 1.7). Above this Virgen de Loreto, a lovely painted scene (figure 1.9) shows young Jesús working together with María and José in the carpenter's workshop. These two central altar icons are flanked by paintings of saints and bas-relief angels framed in gold leaf. The regal white-skinned, European-looking Virgen de Loreto (figure 1.8), golden-crowned and wise, holds a similarly crowned Christ child, two fingers of his right hand raised in benediction, the left hand holding the blue orb of the world.

An older pair of Virgin and Christ child statues, *escultura para vestir* (sculpture to be dressed), draped in blue and white velour tunics, can be found on the modern retablo (figure 1.11) of the side chapel to the right of the main altar, opposite the sacristy. Here stands the original seventeenth-century Virgen de Loreto wooden statue (figure 1.10), the one brought ashore by Padre Salvatierra himself in 1697. This Indian-looking Virgin and the Christ child she holds wear humble straw peasant sombreros. Below the Virgin and Christ child, pinned into a maroon cushion, are a series of *milagros*, miracles requested by supplicants in the form of metal cutouts of body organs, the parts needing to be cured.

Across the street from the church stands a large bronze bust of Padre Salvatierra (figure 1.3). An arched gateway northeast of the church leads through an open walled patio to parochial offices and a separate entry to the chapel with the original Our Lady of Loreto statue. An L-shaped adobe building with arcaded porches, connected to the southwest front of the church and in the rear to a retaining wall, seals off the large, private church courtyard. Inside this plaza stands a wooden rotary wheel once used for bringing up water from the church well. This L-shaped building houses the priest and the historical museum. The INAH historical museum displays many eighteenth-century artifacts, paintings, and sculptures that once graced the Nuestra Señora de Loreto church.

1.2. West wall, side entry, and main courtyard.

1.3. Bronze bust of Jesuit padre Juan María de Salvatierra, located across the pedestrian mall opposite the main entry to the church.

1.4. Main façade above the entryway: the Virgen de Loreto statue. The choir loft window is below. The inscription underneath reads: "Cabeza y Madre de las Misiones de Baja y Alta California."

.5. Restored main açade of the Loreto hurch.

1.6. Nave with pews and the aisle to the main altar.

1.7. Restored main altar with the glass-encased statue of the Virgen de Loreto.

1.8. Detail, wooden statue: Virgen de Loreto with Christ child, probably an eighteenth-century sculpture.

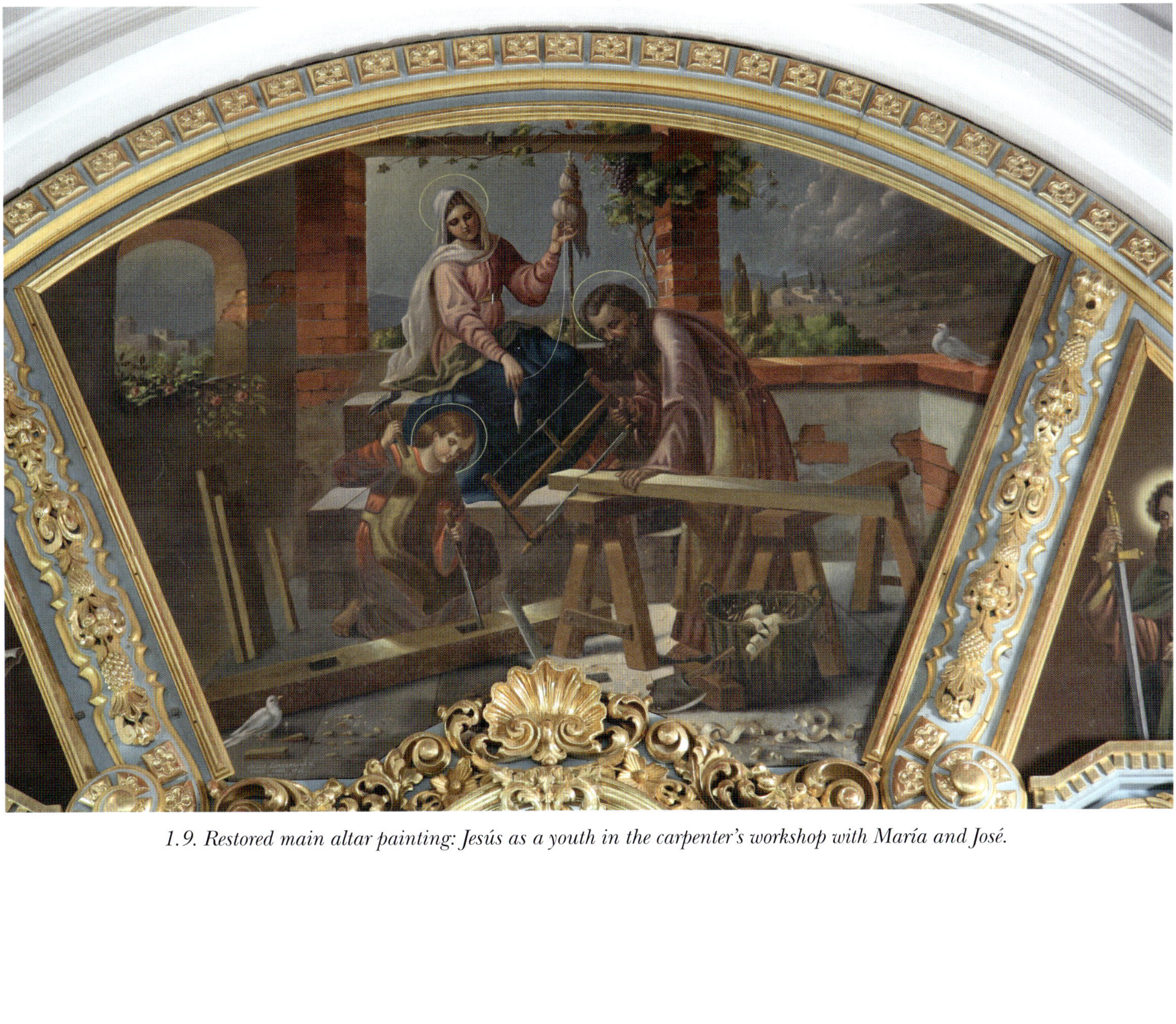

1.9. Restored main altar painting: Jesús as a youth in the carpenter's workshop with María and José.

1.10. Detail, Virgen de Loreto (the seventeenth-century original) and Christ child statues, east side chapel off the main altar.

1.11. Virgen de Loreto statue mounted in a noncolonial retablo in the east chapel off the main altar.

1.12. East side chapel off the entryway: crucifix and Nuestra Señora de los Dolores.

1.13. West side chapel, detail, sculpture of Christ scourged.

1.14. Main entry, choir loft, and side entryways off the nave.

2.1. The road to San Javier above Rancho Las Parras looking back to the Sea of Cortés.

Misión San Francisco Javier Viggé Biaundó, 1699

The San Javier Mission church, situated in a broad, well-watered canyon against a backdrop of sheer cliffs, lies in the Sierra de la Giganta 23 miles southwest of Loreto. Italian padre Francisco María Piccolo founded the first San Javier in 1699. The mission was dedicated to San Francisco Javier, cofounder of the Society of Jesus, the priest who spread Roman Catholicism to India and Asia in the sixteenth century. The site of today's church was relocated a few miles downstream from San Javier Viejo by Padre Juan de Ugarte in 1702. San Javier's mission flourished for nearly a century before being abandoned in 1817. Cochimí Indians who inhabited the original location called their settlement Viggé and the nearby spring Biaundó. The annual feast of Baja's San Francisco Javier Viggé Biaundó and the fiesta of San Francisco Xavier del Bac in Tucson, Arizona, celebrate the same saint on December 3.

The signed turnoff to San Javier Mission is located about 2 miles south of Loreto off the Transpeninsular Highway, Mexico Highway #1. Traveling this same highway from Ciudad Constitución in the south, it takes two hours (90 miles) to reach the turnoff point. The precipitous dirt track that twists dangerously over the passes has recently been paved. It takes an easy hour of driving to get to the mission from this turnoff. At several spots during the ascent, looking back through the mountains, it's possible to catch a glimpse of the Sea of Cortés (figure 2.1). San Javier is probably the best-preserved church in Baja, close to being in its original condition with minimal restoration. It is arguably blessed with the most spectacular panorama of all the missions.

Along the winding road to San Javier, pockets of date palms rise up from canyon water catchments. Passing by Rancho Las Parras and the impassable turnoff via the old Camino Real to Misión San José de Comondú, the road levels out through thickets of mesquite trees. In the approach to San Javier, the narrow canyon opens into a broad expanse one-half mile across. San Javier Canyon and the dirt road that continues through it, beyond San Javier village and the church, winds 50 miles before connecting with Mexico Highway #53 by the Pacific coast. Rimmed by immense cliffs with lava rocks cascading down, the lower canyon slopes are blanketed by cardón and organ pipe cacti and paloverde trees. During the *cabalgata,* the cavalcade of horsemen riding to San Javier in honor of the saint's day fiesta, the Fiestas de San Francisco Javier (December 1–4), the way gets jammed with scores of horses and support vehicles. Entering San Javier village via the cobblestone avenue before the mission, an eighteenth-century monumental iron cross points the way there.

San Javier village, with a population of around one hundred inhabitants, is ringed with orchards and fields. Jesuit-era irrigation canals are still in use. This was the site of Baja California's first vineyards, planted by Padre Ugarte in 1710, and ranchers and growers still cultivate the fertile canyon flatlands with date palms, citrus trees, figs, olives, plums, pomegranates, avocados, and onions, along with individual vegetable and flower gardens. The town's only café, La Palapa, which offers basic food and drink, also rents simple rooms for overnighters. During the Fiesta of San Javier, a four-day celebration featuring a carnival, food, music, and processions of the saint (figure 2.12), with colorful matachines and a Yaqui deer dancer (figure 2.6), hundreds of travelers converge on the mission. Excellent camping spots with some facilities can be rented in the orchards south of town.

The baroque church of San Francisco Javier Viggé Biaundó (figures 2.2, 2.3) impresses by its size, beauty, and masterful workmanship. It's quite a marvel that this exquisite church, erected with gray-colored blocks of cut volcanic stone during the tenure of Spanish padre Miguel del Barco from

2.2. San Javier church looking south.

1744 to 1758, exists in such an isolated place. The San Javier church is designed in the form of a Latin cross and spans a length of 125 feet. Opposing side altars 60 feet apart and 20 feet in width transect the nave to form the crossbar of the cruciform pattern. The nave stretches 21 feet in width, while the vaulted ceilings ascend to 40 feet, the main dome reaching 45 feet in height.

The main entrance to San Javier faces due north, the church also offering two accessory side entryways. The façade displays architectural details only over the entry, up to the arched tympanum, and around the open window that gives light to the choir loft. Ornate stonework (figure 2.5) of the church's east and west faces is prominently displayed above and around each doorway. These sculptural details in relief, some of them Moorish, reveal exquisitely fitted arches, columnar pieces, crosses, oculi (circular windows), and parapet finials that highlight unplastered stone walls. On San Javier's northeast corner rises the square bell tower (figure 2.4) with its six bronze bells. The white cupola of the tower reaches the height of 65 feet. To the rear of the church are attached four large rooms, entered from within through the east-side sacristy. Two more west-side rooms are connected to these four back spaces through a small intermediate patio. The six large rooms were built for storage and to house the priest and his guests.

At fiesta time the great San Javier church is festooned outside and in with colored streamers (figure 2.8). Sunlight floods the interior from huge lateral windows. A constant stream of humanity passes down the aisle to the altar. Sounds of happy

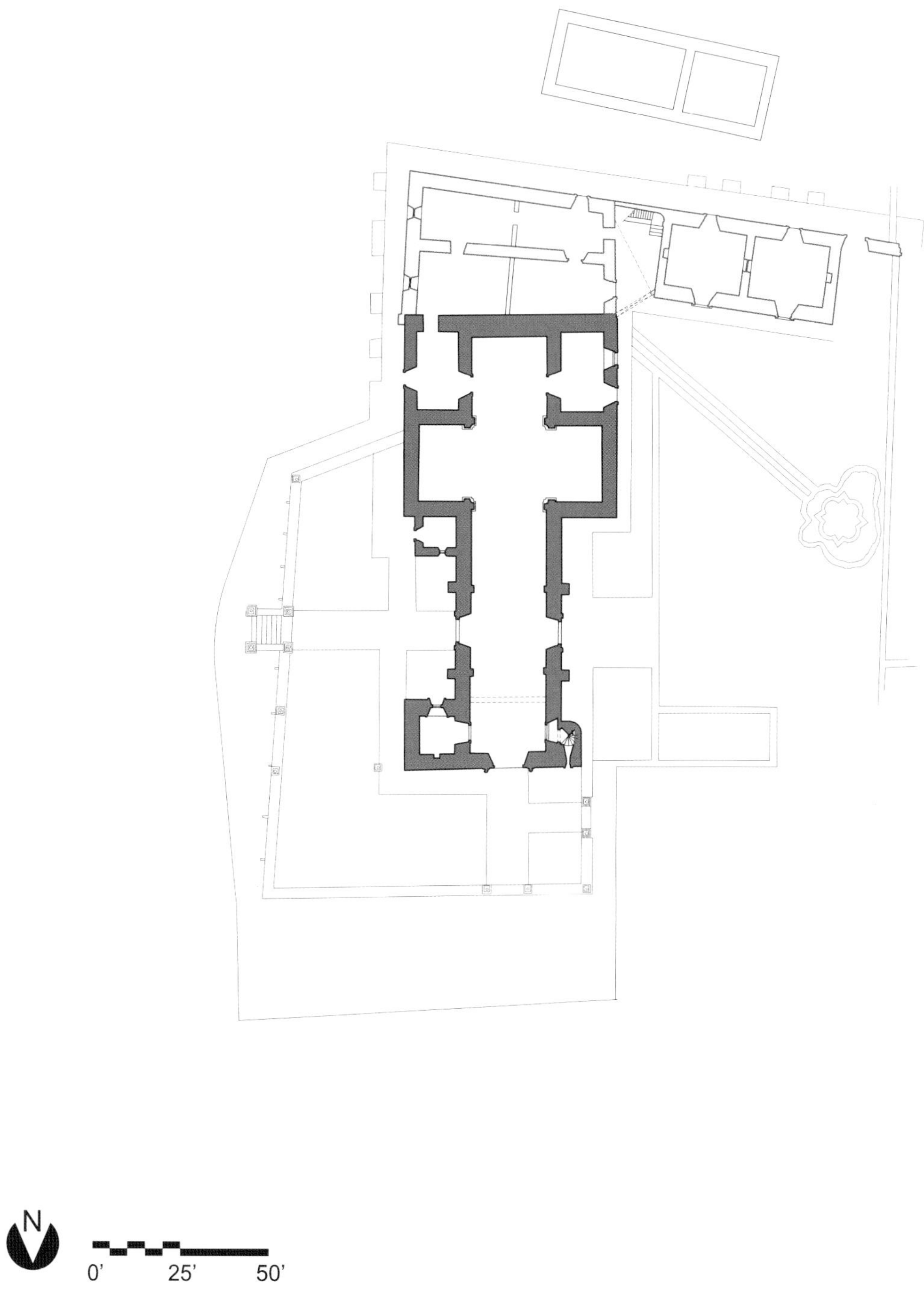

Misión San Francisco Javier Viggé Biaundó

greetings and whispered prayers fill the church. People come to touch the statue of San Francisco Javier (figure 2.11), set down for the fiesta from its altar niche, placed to one side above the communion balustrade. A sea of yellow votive candles flickers across the east wing altar floor. Those who completed the pilgrimage to San Javier in 2009 were blessed to attend the saint's day mass and receive communion (figure 2.13) offered by Miguel Angel Alba Díaz (figure 2.7), bishop of Ensenada. Over the past several years, this beloved bishop has traveled far and wide, presiding over religious observations at Baja California's important Roman Catholic mission festivals.

On either side of the main entry, grilled double wooden doors stand ajar. The east doorway leads to the spiral staircase of the bell tower, the west one to the choir loft. The church floor is paved with hewn blocks of gray stone. Supported by arched columns edged in beige quarry stone, five circular dome vaults rise in succession down the length of the church, one vault above the choir loft, three across the nave ceiling, and one over the main altar. At both ends of the space that transects the nave and dome to form the Latin cross stand two separate gilded altar screens. The two eighteenth-century retablos face north, in the same direction as the main altar. The west-side retablo contains a painted wooden sculpture of San Ignacio de Loyola in the center niche, surrounded by eleven oil paintings of religious personages (figure 2.9). The east-side retablo displays in its central niche a dressed wooden statue of Nuestra Señora de los Dolores. On either side of this statue are three empty slots where paintings once looked out (these six missing canvases are perhaps being restored). Above and below the Nuestra Señora de los Dolores sculpture are two small restored paintings: the crucified Christ and the white handkerchief of Veronica displaying the face of Christ scourged.

In the niche of the main altar screen rests the eighteenth-century painted wooden figure of San Francisco Javier. Eight beautifully restored eighteenth-century oil paintings on canvas arc around this statue (figure 2.10). The painting immediately above, depicting three bearded Christlike figures seated together, represents the Holy Trinity: the Father, the Son, the Holy Ghost. The painting on top of that one shows a winged San Miguel Arcángel. To either side of the statue are stacked three paintings of saints: top down from the left, San Luis Gonzaga, San Joaquín, and San José y el Niño con la Cruz; top down from the right, San Antonio, Santa Ana, and San Pablo. Below the San Javier statue rests a miniature painting of El Sagrado Corazón de Jesús (the Sacred Heart of Jesus) ringed by seven angel faces. During the San Francisco Javier Fiesta, local women daily set fresh flower bouquets on the white linen-covered table before the altar and on the floor all around it. At night they light the candelabras to illuminate the church.

2.3. San Javier church looking east.

2.4. San Javier church tower looking northeast.

2.5. East-side façade of San Javier: a Moorish arch over the entry.

2.6. Matachín dancers leading the procession of San Javier during the Fiesta de San Javier.

2.7. Padre Miguel Angel Alba Díaz, bishop of Ensenada, at the west-side entry to San Javier.

2.8. Looking down the nave toward the main altar during the Fiesta de San Javier.

2.9. Oil painting detail of Santa Rosa de Lima holding the Christ child. From the retablo dedicated to San Ignacio de Loyola in the west side chapel.

2.10. Restored main altar screen with a wooden statue of San Javier and paintings. Two paintings hang above the statue of San Javier, one with three figures that represent the Holy Trinity and the other of San Miguel Arcángel. The three paintings to the left, from the top down, depict San Luis Gonzaga, San Joaquín, and San José y el Niño con la Cruz. The three paintings to the right, from the top down, depict San Antonio, Santa Ana, and San Pablo.

2.11. Main altar patron saint's image from the eighteenth century. San Javier is placed on the left balustrade during the Fiesta de San Javier.

2.12. Procession of San Javier exiting the church during the Fiesta de San Javier.

2.13. Communion mass of San Javier during the Fiesta de San Javier, December 3, 2009.

3.1. View looking west from the Santa Rosalía church grounds, including palm groves along the Río Mulegé toward the Sierra de la Giganta.

Misión Santa Rosalía de Mulegé, 1705

The mission church of Santa Rosalía de Mulegé lies west of the coastal town of Mulegé, just off the Transpeninsular Highway. Situated on a bluff overlooking the Mulegé River with its lush grove of date palms (figure 3.1), the mission was founded in 1705 by Spanish padre Juan Manuel de Basaldúa at the Cochimí ranchería known as Mulegé. The church was dedicated to Santa Rosalía, the twelfth-century patron saint of Palermo, Sicily, native city of Padre Piccolo, who with Padre Basaldúa had chosen the mission site two years earlier. The festival of Santa Rosalía is held on September 4.

Mulegé can be easily reached on Mexico Highway #1 from Loreto in the south, 85 miles (two hours) away, or from Santa Rosalía in the north, 40 miles (one hour) away. With a population of four thousand, the well-known tourist destination offers modest hotels, restaurants, nice beaches, boating, and sport fishing and is one of central Baja California's jumping-off places to explore prehistoric cave paintings. Positioned at the entrance to the beautiful Bahía de Concepción, Mulegé exists because of its verdant palm-lined Arroyo Santa Rosalía, better known as Río Mulegé, the largest river in Baja.

The present Misión Santa Rosalía (figures 3.2, 3.11), built of thickly mortared dark volcanic stone, was begun in the 1750s by Spanish padre Francisco Escalante and finished in 1766. This building replaced an earlier adobe church destroyed by the hurricane of 1717, which set back mission productivity by washing away topsoil from the fields. With smallpox decimating the neophyte population, the mission was finally abandoned in 1828. The main church entrance faces southeast at 140 degrees. The utilitarian-looking Santa Rosalía, with its 50-foot-high bell tower (figure 3.4), appears more a fortress than a church. Exterior detailing exists only in the light-colored quarry-stone fittings around doorways and windows and with six white finials prominent on the parapet wall. The rectangular church of Santa Rosalía is adjoined at the back by a longer western wing, thus forming an L-shaped building (figure 3.3).

The church gallery (figure 3.5) reaches approximately 70 feet in length. This large room with a stone floor, formed by bare stone walls 3 feet thick, with its arched doorways, windows, and niches, measures about 18 feet across the nave. The church's arched ceiling vault reaches nearly 30 feet in height. Only the ceiling and wall behind the altar are plastered. A choir loft with an outside stairway access rises over the entryway. Santa Rosalía's narrower, lower-roofed west wing, about 120 feet in total length, entered off the main altar and from several outside doorways, is connected with passages through three intersecting rooms, the sacristy, priest quarters, and chapel. The recently remodeled chapel (figure 3.10), its pure white plastered walls illuminated by shafts of sunlight coming in through arched doors and windows, possesses more charm than the main gallery. During December 2009, Don Alfredo Robles Regalado of Loreto, the Baja Sur restoration project foreman, and his crew (figure 3.9) were finishing touch-up plastering around the main altar (figure 3.8). Don Alfredo expressed enthusiasm at having worked the last eighteen years in helping restore the mission churches of Baja California Sur.

At one time, Misión Santa Rosalía de Mulegé's interior walls were graced with many beautiful oil paintings of religious scenes, various saints, and portraits of the mission's founders. Unfortunately, none of these paintings remain today. Of Santa Rosalía's sculptural art, only a few genuine eighteenth-century Jesuit pieces can be found on display inside the church. Above the main altar niche hangs a small painted wooden eighteenth-century statue of Christ crucified. Below this crucifix, inside the central altar niche stands a statue of Santa Rosalía under a pillared canopy (figure 3.6). She wears a flowered wreath and a brown robe and holds a cross and rosary in her right hand. This is not the original patron saint sculpture, although the four spiraled gold and white columns holding up the *baldaquín* (canopy) are indeed from the eighteenth century.

Inside the west lateral niche of the main church, dressed in a red velour robe, stands a wooden statue of Christ scourged. This sculpture, like the one of Santa Rosalía, was produced at a much later date, possibly in the late nineteenth century. Attached to opposite walls of the main gallery protrude two spherical stone-chiseled fonts for blessed water; these are from the Jesuit period. Two eighteenth-century sculptures brought to Mulegé by the Jesuits, the original wooden statue of Santa Rosalía (figure 3.7) and one of Nuestra Señora de los Dolores, are located in opposing niches of the side chapel annex. The lovely Santa Rosalía statue is found protected inside a glass case. Presented as a lovely young woman, Santa Rosalía wears a crown of flowers and a brown robe. She holds a book and rosary in her left hand, and her right hand is raised in benediction.

Misión Santa Rosalía de Mulegé

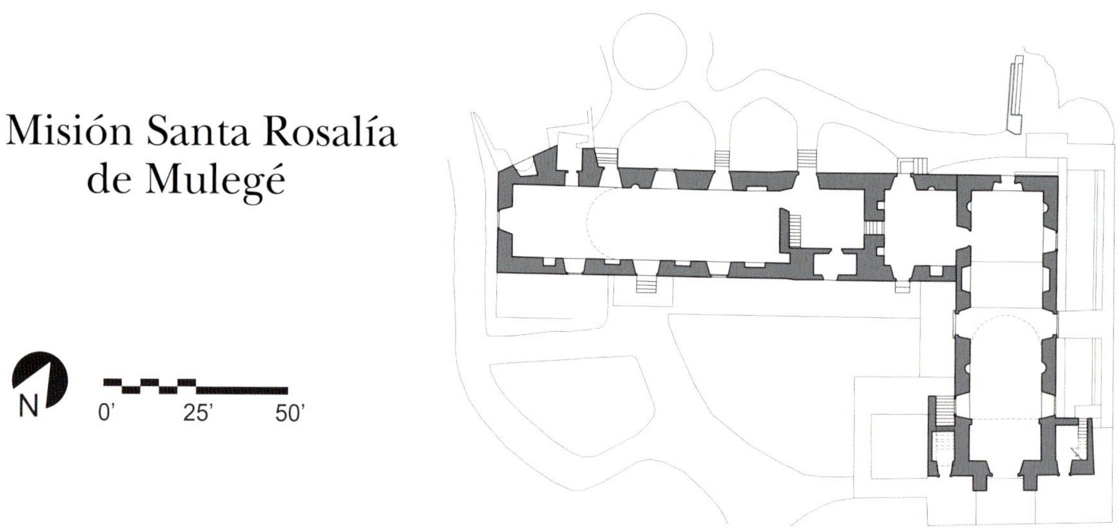

3.2. Santa Rosalía church looking north.

3.3. Santa Rosalía church looking east.

3.4. Santa Rosalía bell tower.

3.5. Main church gallery looking down the nave to the altar.

3.6. Patron saint's image of Santa Rosalía on the main altar, wooden sculpture, probably from the nineteenth century, covered by a baldaquín supported on columns salvaged possibly from an earlier baroque retablo.

3.7. Detail, original eighteenth-century main altar statue of Santa Rosalía de Mulegé located in a glass case in a north alcove of the chapel gallery.

3.8. Restoration plastering around the main altar.

3.9. Restoration crew of Don Alfredo Robles Regalado inside the Mulegé chapel.

3.10. Chapel with arcades and pews.

3.11. Pickup truck passing the Santa Rosalía church.

4.1. San José de Comondú Canyon looking west.

Misión San José de Comondú, 1708

The site of San José de Comondú Mission lies in the heart of the Sierra de la Giganta, 50 miles due west of Loreto. The mission chapel nestles among the trees along a quiet village lane at the upper end of San José de Comondú Canyon (figure 4.1). Because of its constant natural spring and good land, thought to be an ideal place for growing a wide variety of crops, the Jesuits relocated the mission to this oasis in 1737. The original site, San José de Comondú Viejo, established by the Spanish padre Julián de Mayorga in 1708, briefly flourished 15 miles to the northeast. Comondú was the place-name given to this seasonally occupied ranchería by Cochimí nomads. The Jesuit mission was dedicated in the name of San José, husband of María, mother of Jesucristo. The feast day of San José de Comondú is celebrated on March 19.

The best way to get to San José de Comondú is from the Pacific side of Baja via Ciudad Insurgentes. The crossroad town of Ciudad Insurgentes can be reached on the Transpeninsular Highway, Mexico Highway #1, from Loreto in the north, 75 miles (two hours) away, or from Ciudad Constitución in the south, 16 miles (thirty minutes) away. Because of its amenities as an important agricultural center, Ciudad Constitución, a city of fifty thousand, offers the best staging place for a trip to San José de Comondú. After passing through Ciudad Insurgentes, continue north for 40 miles (one hour) on paved Mexico Highway #53. After the marked Francisco Villa settlement, turn northeast at the signed San José de Comondú turnoff, which heads east toward the Sierra de la Giganta. It takes one hour to get to the mission from here. The 25-mile dirt track, which is finally being paved, crosses open desert and slowly rises into the lush recesses of San José de Comondú Canyon, meandering first through San Miguel de Comondú village.

It is also possible to reach San José de Comondú from San Javier Mission, though it's a jarring trip. Departing San Javier to the southwest through Presa Vieja, crossing and recrossing the San Javier Canyon stream to Las Bajadas, it takes two hours over the dusty 50-mile-long washboard road to get to Mexico Highway #53. From San Javier it used to be possible to arrive at San José de Comondú over the mountains in a more direct path, just 25 miles away via the old Camino Real. This road is currently impassable.

According to Don José Jesús Ceseña, the elderly caretaker of the San José de Comondú church, there are 350 residents of the twin Comondú pueblos, San José and San Miguel. Don José and his wife live in the center of town, just a three-minute walk from the mission grounds. They operate a small store and rent out two cottages for overnight guests. There are no restaurants or other commercial places to stay in the area. The shaded avenue of quaint homes that forms San José de Comondú village runs down the center of a one-quarter-mile wide, steep-walled, red-rock canyon fed by a natural freshwater spring located in the heights above. Mesquite and paloverde trees and cardón and organ pipe cacti cover the hillsides of San José de Comondú Canyon. Coursing through the canyon bottomland, dense stands of date palms and clumps of reeds rise along the main road, which parallels the flowing stream.

The terraced fields, orchards, and backyard gardens surrounding San José Comondú still receive water channeled through irrigation ditches and holding tanks laid out by the Jesuits over 250 years ago. In order to create fields for plowing, Indian laborers packed up soil dug out from arroyo side pockets, spreading the rich earth across leveled, rock-cleared areas. During the mission period, along with practicing animal husbandry, the priests and their neophytes grew wheat, corn, sugarcane, and even bananas. Eventually, missionary cultivators discovered that the local earth and terrain were best suited for orchards and vineyards. Many of today's inhabitants of San José and San Miguel de Comondú pursue traditional cattle ranching, while a few individuals run goats and make goat cheese. Local folk still harvest date palms, fig trees, oranges, limes, pomegranates, olives, and avocados and make wine. Alongside their vegetable gardens, they grow roses, marigolds, poinsettias, and geraniums.

The first San José de Comondú mission church, built of sun-dried adobes, was finished by Padre Mayorga in 1717. With its well going dry and epidemics rampant, Padre Mayorga decided in 1736 to relocate the Comondú mission and neophytes farther south to a wider, better-watered canyon. This canyon oasis already contained two prosperous Cochimí settlements, visitas known as San Miguel and San Ignacio. At first San Miguel de Comondú was chosen as headquarters, but by 1737 German padre Francisco Javier Wagner, installed as the new priest, had moved the mission upstream 2 miles to San Ignacio, this site and the canyon being renamed San José de Comondú. San Miguel and Comondú Viejo then became the satellite visiting stations. San José de Comondú Mission was abandoned in 1827.

The only remaining structure of the once-extensive San José de Comondú complex is the stone chapel (figure 4.2), erected in the mid-1750s, possibly built before the principal church gallery. The ruins of the main church were knocked down in 1936. Behind the church and chapel were located a large open courtyard ringed by neophyte apartments, the kitchen, and various storage rooms. The entrance to this beautiful beige and gray stone-block chapel faces northwest at 320 degrees. The rectangular, flat-roofed edifice spans a length of 75 feet and a width of 25 feet, its barrel-vaulted interior of small cut stones reaching a height of about 25 feet. The chapel (figures 4.3, 4.14) possesses several unique and interesting architectural features—turret buttresses supporting its backside façade corners, a cloverleaf window over the main portal, arched side windows, cannonlike stone drain pipes (figure 4.12), and two small stone crosses in relief above side entryways. The interior of the chapel (figures 4.4, 4.13), plastered only on the wall behind the altar, displays marvelous stonework all around. A wooden crucifix hangs midway down from the open, simple altar. Below and to the left side, raised on a table decorated with plastic flowers, stands the original eighteenth-century haloed wooden statue of San José (figure 4.5). He holds the infant Jesús in one hand, a stalk of flowers in the other. To the altar's right emanates a crowned sculpture of Santa María (figure 4.6) dressed in pure white.

Built in front of the chapel and attached to it through the north portal was the east end of the main church. This grand church, Baja California's largest, built of precisely fit stone, measured 145 feet in length, 50 feet in width, and 30 feet in height. Austrian padre Francisco Inama designed and oversaw the construction of San José de Comondú's church and chapel between 1754 and 1762. The main church's three-aisled, triple barrel-vaulted nave was laid out on an east–west axis, supported in the center by two parallel rows of eight arched pillars. The main entry, which passed under the choir loft, faced west, while three sumptuously decorated altars with a spectacular central gilded retablo stood at the east end of the church. Two double-door accessory entrances opened at the center of the church on its north and south sides. Flanking these two entryways stood opposing heraldic pillars, four in all, each mounted by flamed finials chiseled from stone. Over the main entrance and below the choir loft window was affixed a plaque of the Villapuente coat of arms, the Spanish noble family who financed the mission. The flat-roofed church had no bell tower, the bells being stationed separately outside the church. Although early twentieth-century photographs show an imposing, austere exterior, eighteenth-century Jesuit and Franciscan reports praised San José de Comondú's lavishly decorated baroque interior.

Restoring a ruined eighteenth-century church such as San José de Comondú merited little concern during the 1930s, a time of serious religious persecution in Mexico. Needing stones to erect his own mansion and a public school, Gen. Juan Domínguez, governor of Baja California Sur Territory from 1935 to 1937, dynamited the remains of San José de Comondú's main church in 1936. Fortunately, the chapel was left standing, later to be beautifully restored. Salvaged eighteenth-century Jesuit artifacts from the destroyed church include oil paintings of the saints (figures 4.7, 4.8), the previously mentioned wooden sculptures of San José and Santa María, an alabaster baptismal font (figure 4.9), flamed stone finials (figure 4.11), polished wooden pews, and three bronze bells (figure 4.10), one dated 1697. All are on display inside the chapel.

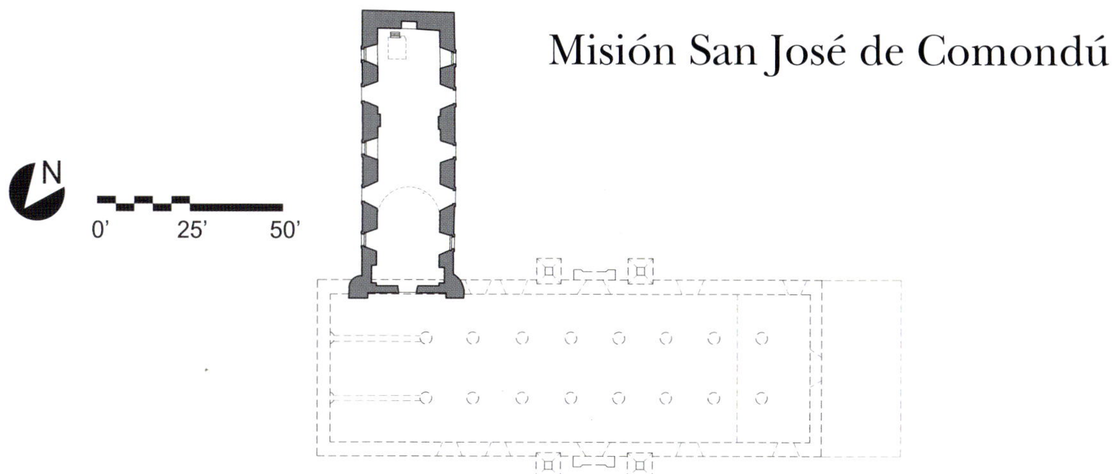

4.2. San José de Comondú chapel looking southeast.

4.3. Chapel entry and main façade. The main church gallery, destroyed in 1936, was connected to the front of this chapel by the southeast side of the main altar.

4.4. Chapel gallery looking toward the main altar with a wooden crucifix and statues of San José and Santa María.

4.5. Detail, San José y el Niño Jesús, wooden sculptures from the altar of the main church, probably from the eighteenth century.

4.6. Detail, Santa María, original wooden sculpture from the altar of the destroyed main church.

4.7. Restored oil painting of San Antonio de Padua, from the main church.

4.8. Restored oil painting of San Luis Gonzaga from the main church.

4.9. Alabaster baptismal font from the main church.

4.10. The bronze bells that hung outside the main church. The bell at the left bears the date 1697.

4.11. Finial flame, one of four stone sculptures from the main church. It was originally mounted on an exterior heraldic stone column.

4.12. Cannon drainage pipe, west-side roof of the chapel.

4.13. Chapel interior looking toward the main entryway.

4.14. San José de Comondú chapel, east-side wall. There is a turret buttress against the corner of the façade.

5.1. San Ignacio church looking to the northeast.

Misión San Ignacio de Kadakaamán, 1728

Its white façade gleaming in the sun, Misión San Ignacio's stately baroque church (figure 5.2) dominates the main plaza of San Ignacio town. The oasis of San Ignacio lies in a valley between the southern Sierra de San Francisco and the northern Sierra de la Giganta. Blessed with a deep natural spring, the town exists because of its narrow freshwater lake, the only natural lake in Baja California. Turning off Mexico Highway #1, the road to town meanders by the lake and passes through dense stands of date palms before entering the town of San Ignacio. The Cochimí called this place Kadakaamán, or Arroyo el Carrizal, Arroyo of Reeds. San Ignacio de Kadakaamán was established in January 1728 by Mexican Jesuit padre Juan Bautista de Luyando. He dedicated the mission to San Ignacio de Loyola (Saint Ignatius of Loyola), founder of the Jesuit Society. San Ignacio celebrates its annual fiesta the last week of July. The feast day is July 31.

Tranquil San Ignacio, with a population of four thousand, can be easily reached from Loreto by the Transpeninsular Highway via Mulegé and Santa Rosalía, 170 miles (four hours) away. To get to San Ignacio from Guerrero Negro on the Pacific side, it's a 90-mile (two-hour) drive. San Ignacio's church overlooks the lovely plaza shaded by Indian laurel trees; the other sides are occupied by restaurants, gift shops, a bed and breakfast with a bookstore, and tour guide offices. High-end accommodations can be found near the lake at the Desert Inn (formerly La Pinta). Besides the attraction of its famous church, San Ignacio is a good jumping-off place to see gray whales at Laguna San Ignacio and for tours of the prehistoric rock art in the Sierra de San Francisco, these two areas being part of the Vizcaíno Biosphere Reserve.

Padre Francisco María Piccolo first discovered the Cochimí rancherías of the San Ignacio area during a 1716 scouting expedition. Because of San Ignacio's miracle lake, arable soil, and large resident Indian population, Padre Piccolo knew it was a perfect mission site. Due to a shortage of priests, Padre Luyando did not arrive until 1728. In the following years, several thousand Cochimí were congregated and converted to Christianity by Luyando, the Mexican padre Sebastián de Sistiaga, and his Croatian aide, Padre Fernando Consag. Indian laborers were put to work cultivating the beautiful valley, and San Ignacio fast became the most productive mission in Baja. Neophytes grazed cattle and goats and planted wheat, sugarcane, dates, figs, olives, pomegranates, and garden vegetables. The vineyards of San Ignacio produced a surplus of sweet red wine, such that the padres shipped off jugs to be sold in Guadalajara and Mexico City. Today the people of San Ignacio still harvest the date palms, citrus trees, and private garden plots, while some run cattle in the desert.

The original Jesuit church of San Ignacio de Kadakaamán was built by Padre Sistiaga of sun-dried adobe bricks mounted by a roof of wooden crossbeams, reeds, and palm thatching. According to the Franciscan inventory of 1773, Sistiaga's church was sumptuously decorated on the inside. The Franciscans listed in detail eighteenth-century Jesuit oil paintings, wooden sculptures, books, vestments, and silver candlesticks and chalices. By this time, the stone walls of another church had already risen. The new church (figure 5.1), with its Latin cross design, begun by Padre Consag in the 1750s, would not be completed until 1786.

Padre Consag proved to be an able linguist, learning several Cochimí dialects, one of the qualities that endeared him to the Indians. He and his fellow Jesuits had baptized over two thousand Cochimí at San Ignacio mission by 1758, bringing in people from Isla Cedros and Guaycura territory to the south. Consag also gained fame as the premier explorer and cartographer of Baja California. The Spanish Crown desired territorial expansion, so in 1746 Padre Consag was sent to explore the upper gulf, once again seeking the phantom sea route to connect mainland Sonora with Alta California. In four Nayarit dugout canoes, Consag departed Bahía de los Angeles with six soldiers, local Cochimí and Yaqui boatmen from Sonora. They paddled north up the coast and beyond the tidal bore of the Colorado River. Flanked by mountains in the west and freshwater marshes to the east, Consag knew for certain, as did Francisco de Ulloa and Padre Ugarte before him, that Baja California was a peninsula.

As the Jesuits wanted to found more missions, Consag explored possible sites farther inland. During another expedition in 1747, beyond the Visita San Pablo (also known as Dolores del Norte), which he had established 20 miles to the north of San Ignacio in 1740, Padre Consag discovered a natural spring with good land around it, the future site of Misión Santa Gertrudis de Cadacamán. In 1753 Consag again ventured to the northwest of Baja California to assess resources there. Back in San Ignacio, he laid foundations for the new church and engineered construction of a 3-mile-long dyke to keep flash floods from sweeping away the church and its surrounding fields. Padre Consag died in 1759 and was buried on the mission grounds.

True to Padre Consag's Latin cross design, the church of San Ignacio de Kadakaamán was completed in 1786 by Dominican padre Juan Crisóstomo Gómez. The courtyard of San Ignacio, open at the front, is enclosed on three sides, by the church to the north, the INAH historical museum on the

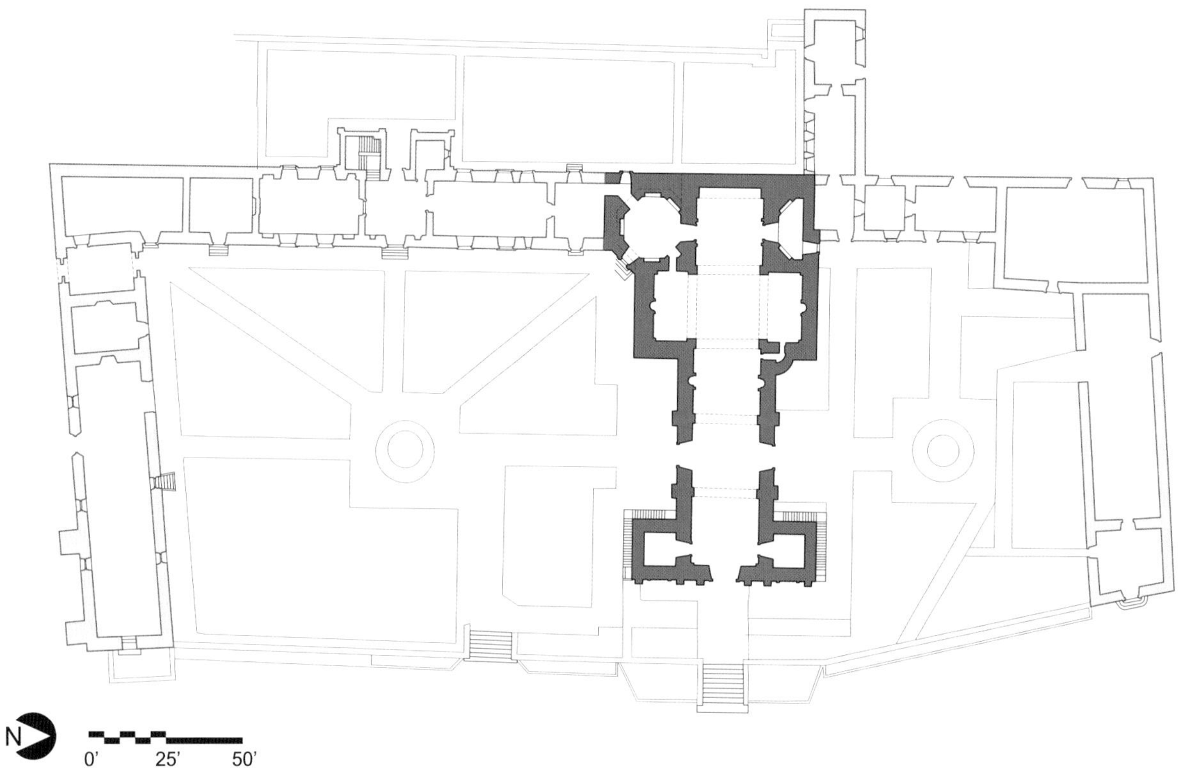

Misión San Ignacio de Kadakaamán

south, and the south-side wing church extension to the rear (figure 5.13), which includes the priest's residence (figure 5.14). The mortared 4-foot-thick church walls, containing massive arched doorways and windows, were laid of cut gray-colored lava block. Only the façade, bell tower, and dome are plastered. A tribute to Dominican architectural achievement, the 60-foot-high bell tower thrusts up from the building's southeastern corner. The whitewashed central dome billows next to it, while four pale finials stand nearby on the parapet wall. The prominent beige-colored stonework decorating the façade in relief (figure 5.3)—the only Baja church embellished in this manner—displays considerable artistry in the Moorish style, especially in the stonework of the arch over the entrance.

Six rectangular engaged columns rise up the front face of the building. A round floral medallion, the Dominican coat of arms, rests in relief above the doorway, and over that, a rectangular window allows light into the choir loft. Between parallel columns, two on either side of the entry, stand four stone saints in their niches: to the left, Santo Domingo and San Pedro; on the right, San Francisco and perhaps San Ignacio. Across the top half of the façade, two pairs of oculi are bracketed by the engaged columns. Emblazoned on the lower half of the façade, left and right of the main doors, above another set of oculi, protrude two heraldic plaques, the Spanish royal coat of arms and the Pillars of Hercules, representing Spain and North Africa.

The main entrance to the beautiful San Ignacio church faces due east, its two exquisitely carved wooden doors each flaunting a gargoyle face (figure 5.12). Inside, the choir loft (figure 5.10), with its wooden banister, rises over the entrance to face the central altar. Opposing doors swing open at either side below the loft: the left-side door goes to the bell tower stairwell, while the right door admits to a small chapel. The choir loft is reached by two separate outside stairways, the north-side steps mounted with a cloverleaf-patterned stone cross (figure 5.11). Tightly set stones make up the church floor. Lateral double wooden doors access both flanks of the church into the center of the nave. Dimensions of the church are 125 feet in length, 63 feet of width across the façade, and 21 feet of width across the nave. The interior space that transects the nave and dome before the altar to form the Latin cross spans 40 feet in length, 20 feet in width. Both end walls of the aisle crossing the nave exhibit elaborate secondary altars. Three domical vaults reach nearly 40 feet in height, while the dome (figure 5.8) spanning the crux of the church ascends to nearly 45 feet.

Misón San Ignacio de Kadakaamán's principal altar (figure 5.4), consecrated to San Ignacio de Loyola, reflects baroque splendor, its delicately carved and gilded framework, the sculpture, and the oil paintings dating from the late eighteenth-century Dominican period. San Ignacio's handsome interior equals that of San Francisco Javier Viggé Biaundó. Inside the central retablo niche glows a painted black and gold wooden statue of San Ignacio (figure 5.5). San Ignacio holds a Jesuit banner in his right hand; his left hand holds an open book printed with the Latin phrase "Ad Majorem Dei Gloriam" (for the greater glory of God), the motto of the Society of Jesus. Seven framed paintings arch around San Ignacio's image in a clockwise direction: San Vicente Ferrer, San José y el Niño con la Cruz, San Pedro y San Pablo, the Virgen del Pilar, an unknown saint, San Juan Bautista, and Santo Tomás de Aquino. Below San Ignacio are two lovely miniature paintings (figure 5.6) of the Sagrado Corazón (Sacred Heart) and Jesús con Símbolos de la Eucaristía (Jesus with symbols of the Eucharist). The sacristies are located on either side of the main altar. On the left stands a wooden statue of the crucified Christ.

Dedicated to La Pasión de Jesús and to La Sagrada Familia, on opposing sides across the nave

5.2. Main façade and bell tower.

stand two gilded altar panels arched around stone niches. La Pasión de Jesús retablo (figure 5.7) on the south lateral wall features a delicate sculpture of Jesus surrounded by nine paintings: five illustrate the trials of Jesus, two paintings above depict Santa Catalina de Alejandría and Santa Inéz, and two portraits below show Santo Domingo de Guzmán and Santa Catalina de Siena. On the north-side lateral wall, La Sagrada Familia retablo features a Virgen de Guadalupe statue surrounded by nine paintings: five illustrate the sacred events of Jesus's family, two paintings above show Santiago Apóstol (Saint James) and Santa María Magdalena, and two portraits below show Saint Pius V and an unknown saint. Off the north lateral wall protrudes a finely carved wooden pulpit (figure 5.9), the only one in Baja. On top of the pulpit canopy gestures a statue of La Virgen Inmaculada. A niche next to the pulpit contains a statue of San Martín de Porres, the black saint of humble station much revered in Latin America. By the north accessory entry stands a lovely half-round reddish brown sandstone baptismal font with a half shell and gargoyle spout backing. A winged angel hangs from the center of the principal dome, while other stone angel faces peer down from the ceiling.

5.3. Stone stairs leading to the double doors of the main entryway.

5.4. Restored main altar screen, including the central wooden statue of San Ignacio de Loyola with paintings. Clockwise from lower left: San Vicente Ferrer, San José y el Niño con la Cruz, San Pedro y San Pablo, the Virgen del Pilar, an unknown saint, San Juan Bautista, and Santo Tomás de Aquino.

5.5. Wooden sculpture of San Ignacio de Loyola holding the Jesuit banner in gold and black, from the eighteenth century.

5.6. Main altar miniature paintings of the Sagrado Corazón (Sacred Heart) (above) and Jesús con Símbolos de la Eucaristía (Jesus with symbols of the Eucharist) below the statue of San Ignacio.

5.7. Retablo dedicated to La Pasión de Jesús. A wooden sculpture of Jesús, surrounded by restored paintings, is located on the south lateral wall.

5.8. Central dome and arches.

5.9. Carved wooden pulpit with a wooden statue of San Martín de Porres on the north lateral wall of the nave.

5.10. Aisle back up the nave, looking toward the entryway and choir loft. Mina is checking her pictures.

5.11. A stone cloverleaf cross.

5.12. Detail, wooden gargoyle sculpture above the entryway door.

5.13. Main courtyard and southern wing off the rear of the church.

5.14. Entrance to the priest's residence in the main courtyard.

6.1. Church of San Luis Gonzaga and surroundings looking east.

Misión San Luis Gonzaga Chiriyaqui, 1737

The lovely temple of San Luis Gonzaga (figure 6.1), located farthest south of the eight intact Baja California churches, lies 35 miles southeast of Ciudad Constitución off the Transpeninsular Highway, Mexico Highway #1. Looking like it is made of gingerbread, with cream-brown brick trim and a new whitewashed façade, the rustic stone church stands in a shallow basin above an arroyo with a freshwater spring. Because of this perennial spring, a lush grove of date palms flourishes in one of the most sterile desert regions of the peninsula, the Magdalena Plain. Guaycura natives of the early eighteenth century who lived around the waterhole of reeds called the location Chiriyaqui. Today's mission church, finished in 1758 by German padre Juan Jacobo Baegert, was dedicated to the youthful eighteenth-century Italian Jesuit, San Luis Gonzaga (Saint Aloysius Gonzaga). The feast day is celebrated with a fiesta on June 21.

To get to the San Luis Gonzaga Chiriyaqui from Ciudad Constitución, take Mexico Highway #1 south of town for about 10 miles before heading east off the paved highway. Two miles after the village of Villa Morelos, locate the marked San Luis Gonzaga sign and take that road. Coming north from La Paz, it's 125 miles (two and one-half hours) before reaching the turnoff. Proceed on the dusty, bumpy, unpaved road for 25 miles (one hour). The surrounding desert is quite sparse, nothing but desolate space with the Sierra de la Giganta ranging to the east. Finally, just over a rise, a dark green patch of palm trees appears on the horizon—San Luis Gonzaga Chiriyaqui oasis and its pretty little church! Adjacent to the church (figure 6.3) are found the roofless walls of the priest's quarters and mission annex. Across the road from these two structures stands a large yellow building that served as the hacienda company store before the Mexican Revolution.

According to Doña María Higueras, the church caretaker who lives across the street, nine families reside in town. With electrical wires coming in from the highway, the inhabitants are not quite as isolated as it may seem. They have a resident teacher, and the boarding school receives educational television broadcasts via satellite dish. Local action revolves around the small Conasupo, a government-subsidized food store. The townsfolk of San Luis Gonzaga make their living husbanding cattle and goats; they harvest the date palms, collect mesquite firewood, make charcoal from it, run an organic cherry tomato farm, and tend their own vegetable gardens. There are no accommodations for travelers. Overnighters should bring camping equipment, preferably a portable canopy, tent, chairs, table, camping stove, lantern, and, of course, plenty of beer and food.

The Jesuit visita of San Luis Gonzaga Chiriyaqui was first established in 1721 by Mexican padre Clemente Guillén as an outpost to Misión Nuestra Señora de los Dolores Apaté by the Sea of Cortés, 100 miles north of La Paz. Due to Guaycura rebellions and scant productivity of crops, Dolores Apaté was abandoned and replaced by San Luis Gonzaga, which then became a full-fledged mission in 1737 under the direction of German padre Lamberto Hostell. Padre Hostell also founded a new visita, La Pasión (sometimes known as Dolores Chillá), located to the east of San Luis Gonzaga and south of forsaken Dolores Apaté. Two thousand Indians were rotating in attendance at San Luis Gonzaga when Padre Juan Jacobo Baegert arrived in 1751. Due to epidemic diseases, only three hundred souls remained when the mission was abandoned in 1768 by the Jesuit expulsion. These last Guaycura of San Luis Gonzaga were then moved by the Franciscans to Misión Santa Rosa de las Palmas at Todos Santos on the Pacific side.

Padre Baegert's introduction to the mission came in the wake of a hurricane that destroyed the adobe church and residence built by Padre Hostell. The raging torrent had also carried away the mission's cultivated fields. Famous for his acerbic letters describing the ways of naked, godless Guaycura, including the disgust he held for whoremongering Spanish soldiers, Baegert was nevertheless a committed priest. Padre Baegert noted what he called hereditary Guaycura vices—laziness, lying, stealing, the practice of polygamy, and abortion—yet he found himself mystified that the Indians were always laughing and happy. Baegert's linguistic aptitude and keen observations, recorded in nine letters to his brother, could qualify him as Baja's first anthropologist. While ministering to and converting hundreds of Guaycura from surrounding rancherías to the Roman Catholic way of life, Baegert energetically attempted to supervise them in the planting of corn, wheat, and sugarcane and the tending of vineyards, date palms, and beasts of burden.

Padre Baegert began construction of the mortared, uncut sandstone church in 1753. After he located a mason to mount the fired-brick barrel-vaulted ceiling, his lovely temple was finally completed in 1758. The only entrance to San Luis Gonzaga faces due north (figure 6.4). The gabled façade, outlined in brick and flanked by two bell towers (figure 6.8), is plastered white, same as the roof. In relief above the arched double-door entryway are five connected stars and the letters

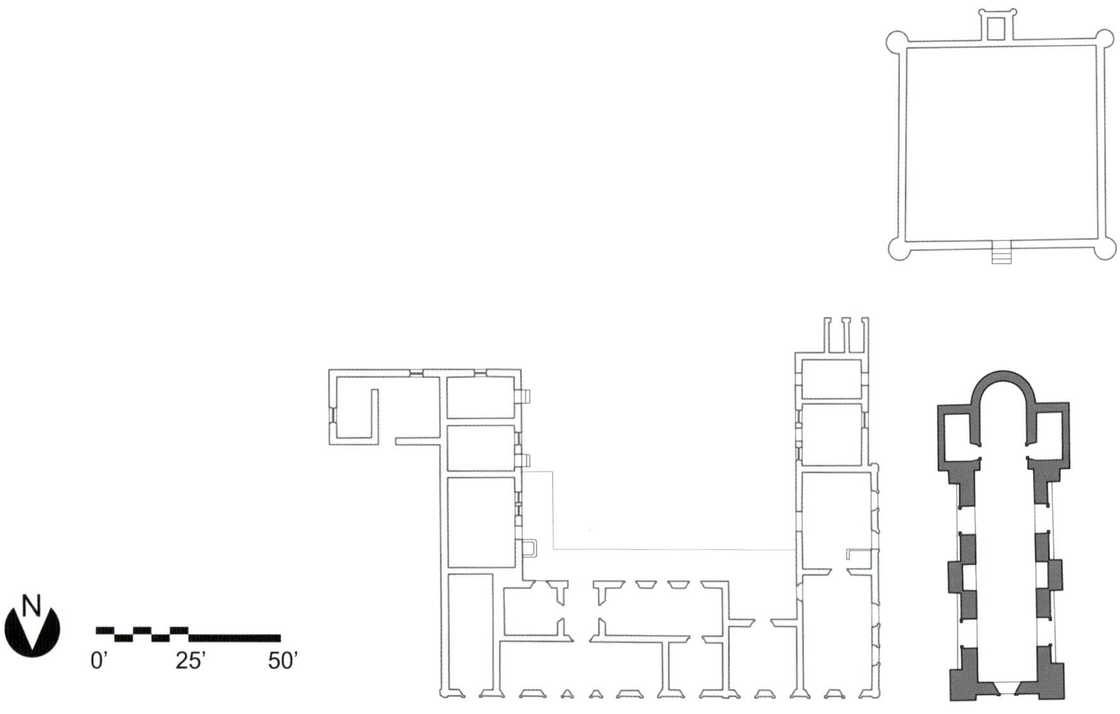

Misión San Luis Gonzaga Chiriyaqui

JHS (IHS) (figure 6.10), "Iesous Hominem Salvator" (Jesus, savior of man), adopted by Ignatius of Loyola as the Jesuit emblem. The outer, unplastered walls receive the support of two buttresses on either side. Balancing east- and west-side sacristies connect off the altar toward the end of the building, while the rear of the church comes together as a unique rounded wall (figure 6.2). A cut-stone swirl-and-leaf pattern (figure 6.9) wraps around each bell tower midway up. Over each of four lateral arched windows runs another floral design of simplicity and beauty. On either side of the roof, above each drainage canal, a carved stone gargoyle face (figure 6.11) looks out over the land. The estimated dimensions of San Luis Gonzaga church are 80 feet total length and 24 feet in width, with 3-foot-thick walls, an 18-foot-wide nave, a 24-foot-high vaulted ceiling, and two 35-foot-high towers, each topped with a wooden cross.

Peering inside the austere church, it's hard not to be impressed by the clean, minimalist interior. Three opposing arched alcoves on the lateral walls, two of them admitting sunlight, beautifully illuminate the church (figure 6.7). Three stone arches mounted off incised capitals transverse the barrel vault, giving decoration to the ceiling and walls. The aisle between two rows of humble pews set on rough-cut stone flooring shows the way to the main altar. On the altar platform and by its alcoves, vases of bright-colored plastic flowers are placed on tables covered in white cloth. Central to the simple altar sanctuary, below a tall, thin crucifix, stands a small, striking, eighteenth-century wooden statue of San Luis Gonzaga (figure 6.6). While holding a crucifix in both hands, the youthful saint wears a blue vestment over a black and white habit. Below the altar are three framed color prints, two of La Virgen de Guadalupe.

According to Padre Baegert's own account, the walls of the new church held ten beautiful oil paintings mounted in gilded frames. A fine wooden statue of Santa María stood central to the altar sanctuary, three paintings hanging behind it, the largest one of San Luis Gonzaga. These paintings and the sculpture of María mentioned by Padre Baegert have long since disappeared. In a niche of the west sacristy rests a small eighteenth-century stone statue of Nuestra Señora de los Dolores.

6.2. West-side view with two buttresses. The sacristy is off the rounded rear of the church.

6.3. Church façade and east wall. The old priest's quarters are next door.

6.4. Entryway with church caretaker, Doña María Higueras.

6.5. The nave looking toward the main altar.

6.6. Detail, main altar wooden sculpture of the patron saint, San Luis Gonzaga, from the eighteenth century.

6.7. The nave looking back toward the entryway.

6.8. East-side bell tower.

6.9. Detail, east wall exterior stonework frieze set into plaster.

6.10. Façade detail, including the emblem of the Society of Jesus.

6.11. A stone carved gargoyle over the west-side roof drainpipe.

7.1. Palm grove and pool in the arroyo below the Santa Gertrudis church.

Misión Santa Gertrudis de Cadacamán, 1751

The church of Santa Gertrudis de Cadacamán lies just inside the southern boundary of Baja California Norte, 50 miles to the north of the town of San Ignacio, beyond the Sierra de San Francisco. Situated on a plateau above a freshwater spring, the simple Santa Gertrudis church of the Dominicans looks across a wide, deep canyon that drains the western slope of the Sierra Aguajito. The mission was founded in 1751 by German Jesuit padre Jorge Retz at the location discovered by Padre Fernando Consag four years earlier. Hundreds of Cochimí Indians from surrounding rancherías were brought in to be baptized and receive religious training while being introduced to the ways of a farming community. The Cochimí called the location Cadacamán, Arroyo of Reeds, the same name, Kadakaamán, as at San Ignacio. Padre Retz dedicated the mission to the thirteenth-century mystic German Benedictine nun Santa Gertrudis la Magna (Saint Gertrude the Great). The mission and church were abandoned in 1822. The feast day of the Santa Gertrudis pilgrimage is held on November 16.

Santa Gertrudis, the most isolated of the eight intact eighteenth-century Baja California missions, can be reached from opposite directions coming off the Transpeninsular Highway, Mexico Highway #1, by way of either San Ignacio or Guerrero Negro. Drive 35 miles northwest from San Ignacio on the paved highway, then go 2 miles beyond the junction toward Bahía de Tortugas. Turn right at the sign indicating Ejido Guillermo Prieto. The dirt track leads north for 22 desolate miles (one hour) to the defunct mining town of El Arco, the junction turnoff to Santa Gertrudis. Coming from Guerrero Negro on Mexico Highway #1, drive southeast for 20 miles and turn east on Mexico Highway #18, then go for 24 miles (one hour) to reach El Arco. In El Arco a marker points the way to Santa Gertrudis. It takes one hour (25 miles) more to reach the Santa Gertrudis oasis, a dusty but fantastic drive through thickets of cardón cacti and yellow-barked elephant trees.

Thick stands of date palms dot the arroyo in the approach to Santa Gertrudis Mission. The meandering road turns down into a grove of huge palms with shaded pools of clear water (figure 7.1). Up the embankment, overlooking the mile-wide floodplain, perches the cream-colored stone church (figures 7.2, 7.3). According to Doña Manuela Urias, who lives near the Santa Gertrudis church, there are seven full-time residents in town. A few cattle ranchers live scattered up and down the canyon. From the spring, irrigation channels run to orchards where date, fig, pomegranate, avocado, citrus, and olive trees are still cultivated. In smaller gardens the locals grow grapes, guavas, bananas, corn, potatoes, squash, melons, herbs, and flowers. Overnight accommodations with bathroom and cold shower but no electricity can be arranged at the hacienda lying west of and below the church. There are many possibilities for camping along the arroyo.

Padre Jorge Retz, the founder of Santa Gertrudis de Cadacamán, ministered to several thousand Cochimí neophytes who congregated to the mission during its first years. While building an adobe church above the floodplain, Retz directed the Indians to clear fields around it and carry up fertile soil from the streambeds below. Along the great arroyo, he had them stake livestock corrals and plant fruit trees to establish the orchards. During drought or when food stores were low, supply ships from Sonora delivered produce to Bahía de San Juan Bautista, 15 miles away by pack trail from Santa Gertrudis. In 1769, the year following Padre Retz's expulsion, Junípero Serra, Franciscan father superior of the California missions, visited Padre Dionisio Basterra, the newly installed priest of Santa Gertrudis. Padre

Basterra celebrated Serra's arrival with great ceremony, including a procession and special mass. In private, Basterra tearfully told Padre Serra of his loneliness as the only European, how he was barely able to cope because of depression and his inability to communicate in the Cochimí tongue.

Baja mission populations declined nearly 30 percent during the first decade of the Dominican period, which began in 1772. The decline was actually due to the smallpox epidemic of 1781–82. This terrible epidemic was introduced into Baja California by infected colonists who arrived at Loreto in the spring of 1781. Especially devastated were the Cochimí of Santa Gertrudis de Cadacamán, whose population declined from 1,700 to 300 souls in twenty years. As the virulence raged up and down the peninsula, the Dominican priests at the San Ignacio de Kadakaamán, San Francisco de Borja Adac, and San Fernando de Velicatá missions chose to practice an immunization procedure first used in New Spain in 1779. This inoculation technique, *variolación*, which transferred pus tapped from ripe smallpox variolas, or pustules, to cuts made between the fingers of healthy persons, saved hundreds of lives at the three missions. Mission burial registers indicate that by the end of 1782, a 20 percent death rate occurred at San Ignacio, 30 percent at San Borja. At Santa Gertrudis, where variolation was rejected, the mission lost 60 percent of its neophytes in two years.

Today's simple, flat-roofed, L-shaped Santa Gertrudis de Cadacamán church, composed of mortared cut quarry-stone facing on rubble, was completed by Dominicans in 1796. To the west of the church can be found the outlines of the original Jesuit adobe, which was abandoned for the newer stone structure. Santa Gertrudis underwent extensive restoration and renovation in the

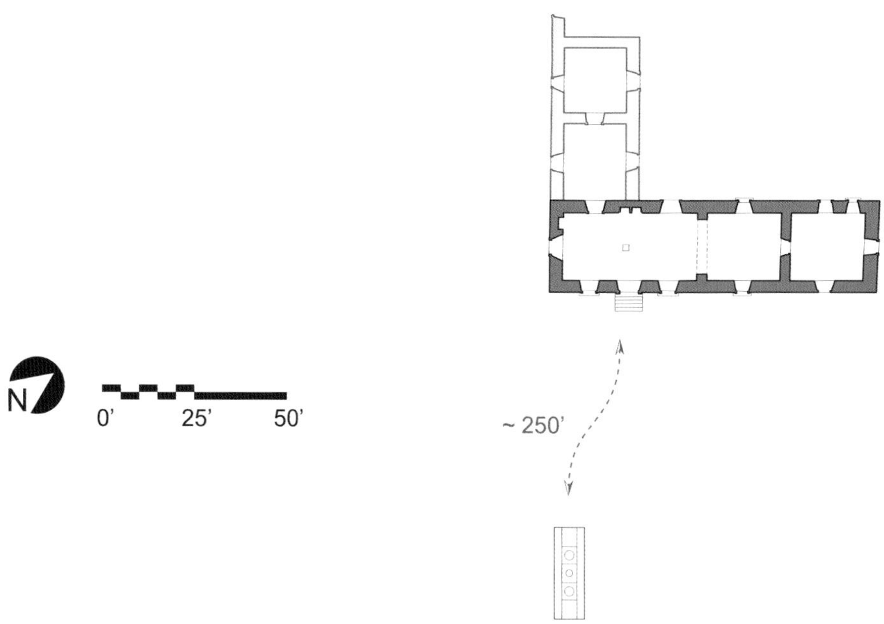

Misión Santa Gertrudis de Cadacamán

1970s and again in 1997. The principal entrance to the Dominican church faces east-southeast at 120 degrees. Two hundred fifty feet to the east of Santa Gertrudis stands the 9-foot-high belfry (figures 7.11, 7.12) hung with three bronze bells, the only church in Baja with a separate bell tower. On the southeast corner of the church rises a small stone cross. Underneath the overhanging parapet run a score of stone drainage canals. On the exterior, the façade of Santa Gertrudis exhibits the baroque aesthetic in detailing only around the entryway (figure 7.4) and the windows and on the steps approaching the church. Cut-stone fluted columns mounted by beacons flank the intricate double-door access, while an incised cross and eight-pointed star rise above. The approximate dimensions of the church are 87 feet in length across the east wall; 74 feet in length on the south wall; 15 feet in height; and about 24 feet in width, 18 feet across the nave. The walls are 3 feet thick.

Entering the church, the supplicant must turn 90 degrees to face the altar. The interior (figure 7.8) is plastered and whitewashed, with detailing found only as ribs of the arched ceiling. Narrow side aisles on either side of the pews lead around to the altar. The recently reconstructed three-niche altar (figure 7.5) of white quarry stone stands off the back wall but is connected to the ceiling to support the roof. Passages around the pillared altar admit to the sacristy behind it. A stone table for presenting the host, a stone pulpit, and a priest's seat complete the modern additions to the church interior. Restored eighteenth-century wooden sculptures grace the three niches of the altar. In the central niche hangs Christ crucified, with an oil portrait of the scourged Christ below a gilt frame mounted by the face of an angel (figure 7.7); in the niche to the left stands La Virgen del Rosario; in the niche to the right, holding a crosier in one hand and an open book in the other, emanates Santa Gertrudis la Magna (figure 7.6), patroness of the mission. In the center of the nave ceiling runs a circular inscription in Latin, "HOC.OPUSCONFECIMEV.DELL.ANNODOMINI MDCCXCVI" (this work I finished in the year of our Lord 1796).

Hanging down from the ceiling near the entry, facing the floor, is a golden sun medallion with the central image of a crouching dog holding a flaming torch in its mouth (figure 7.10). This traditional Dominican symbol represents the dream of Saint Dominic's mother before his birth—the coming of one who would light up the world. By an east-side window stands the original stone baptismal font. Through the west lateral wall opens a second access to the nave. To the rear of the church, a passage opposite the entryway leads to two connected rooms, formerly the priest's quarters, now used for storage and display of religious artifacts. Habits of the three Catholic orders of Baja are draped over hangers: black for the Jesuits, brown for the Franciscans, white for the Dominicans. Within a large Plexiglas case are arranged a number of historical items. The most compelling object inside the case is a small, unretouched, eighteenth-century painting of a white lamb (figure 7.9) resting on an altar, a white flag emblazoned with a red cross positioned behind it—the mystic Lamb of God, symbol of the resurrection. In one corner of the room rests a beautifully painted wood and leather eighteenth-century confessional.

Across the open yard west of the church, near to where the original Jesuit adobe church used to be, a 4-foot-long, 3-foot-high quarry-stone frieze (figure 7.13) of recent vintage goes almost unnoticed. The sculpture depicts a domestic scene that might have happened at Santa Gertrudis two hundred years ago. Under a palm tree in front of Santa Gertrudis church, an Indian woman grinds corn while watching her two daughters play—the only mission monument dedicated to the extinct indigenous people of Baja California.

7.2. Main façade and entryway of the Santa Gertrudis church.

7.3. East-side view of the church.

7.4. Main entrance to the church, Mina Sedgwick before the doorway.

7.5. Main church gallery toward the modern altar of stone. The crucifix is flanked by two wooden statues: on the left is the Virgen del Rosario; on the right is Santa Gertrudis la Magna. Below is a painting of Christ scourged.

7.6. Wooden sculpture of Santa Gertrudis with a crosier, from the eighteenth century.

7.7. Detail, main altar sculpture of an angel.

7.8. Nave looking back over the pews. Main entry to the left.

7.9. Painting of the Lamb of God against a wooden altar niche, with other memorabilia inside a Plexiglas case. The church museum is located in the west wing.

7.10. Detail, underside of canopy, east lateral wall. The crouched dog with a torch in its mouth on a golden sun is the escutcheon of Saint Dominic.

7.11. A bronze bell of Santa Gertrudis.

7.12. Campanile with three bells east of the church.

7.13. Detail, contemporary sculpture of a Cochimí domestic scene of a mother and her two daughters before the Santa Gertrudis church.

8.1. San Borja church, main façade and the extended east wing.

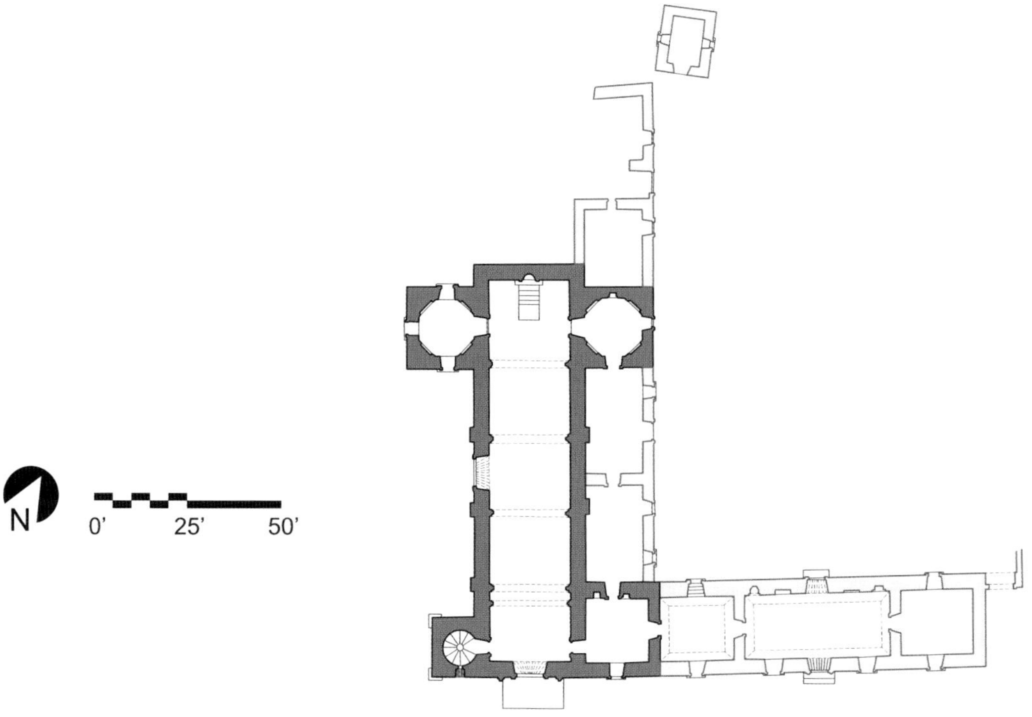

Misión San Francisco de Borja Adac

8.2. West-side view of the church.

8.3. East-wing portal with Mina Sedgwick. Above the doorway, bottom to top: the cross of Alcántara, a Latin cross, and the scallop shell of Saint James.

8.4. Main façade, decorative columns, frieze stonework detailing, and double-door entry with Genaro Monteón.

8.5. Main church gallery looking toward the entryway. The baptismal font is centered in the nave, with the choir loft above.

8.6. Main altar, glass-encased niche containing the wooden statue of the patron saint, San Francisco de Borja. A wooden crucifix hangs above the altar; to the left is a wooden statue of Nuestra Señora de los Dolores; to the right is a wooden statue of the Virgen María.

8.7. A wooden sculpture of San Francisco de Borja with a crucifix and book, from the eighteenth century.

8.8. Frieze detail of main façade above entryway: the Dominican cross of Alcántara, the crossed double-barred patriarchal cross, and a lily stalk, possibly the escutcheon of the House of Borja.

8.9. Baptistery detail, with its recessed, stone-carved wash basin.

8.10. Detail of the caracol, the spiral staircase that leads to the choir loft and bell tower.

8.11. Frontal view of San Borja with caretaker Don Gerardo Monteón.

Looking Back at the Baja California Missions

Eight stone churches from the eighteenth century stand as the only intact Spanish colonial monuments on Baja California. Three of the restored mission churches can be easily found off the Transpeninsular Highway in the comfortable tourist towns of San Ignacio, Mulegé, and Loreto, where one can enjoy the lovely churches and historical museums at leisure, even take lunch at a sidewalk café. Travelers who depart the main highway for Baja California's five remote historic churches will encounter plenty of rough dirt roads. San Borja, Santa Gertrudis, and San Luis Gonzaga are reached by separate lonely tracks that snake across open desert, little-traveled routes terminating at unexpected waterholes surrounded by palm trees. A winding road leads through the western side of the Sierra de la Giganta to San José de Comondú, plunging into a deep valley shaded by huge stands of date palms. Steep ascents to San Javier pass into the eastern side of the Sierra de la Giganta, its canyon a wide expanse dotted with fields and orchards. Each remote site is anchored by the jewel of a stone church. Driving to these missions through the wastes of Baja California, one appreciates the achievement of padres who built these fantastic churches in such faraway, difficult places.

The inspired Jesuit, Franciscan, and Dominican priests who devoted their lives to Baja California began their life's journey in the New World as missionaries, given in marriage to the Catholic Church, forsaking family and homeland. They sailed the Atlantic Ocean in wooden ships, crossing the treacherous waters of the Sea of Cortés to reach the peninsula. Taking few personal effects other than the habits they wore, the priests and their companions walked Baja California over Indian trails, trudging for days to reach the next waterhole. They endured thirst and hunger and lacked shelter. With the relentless sun scorching their backs, the padres beseeched the Lord to deliver his mercy.

Once the padres arrived at the sites selected for their missions, it took a generation or more for the priests to transform Native Americans into Christians, molding them into citizens of mostly self-sufficient agricultural and pastoral communities. Then they were ready to erect permanent churches. The creation of a stone temple in the middle of nowhere was a daunting task. The architect-priests contracted masons and stonecutters from the cities of Nueva España, bringing them to Baja California to build their churches. They organized Indian workers to transport cut quarry-stone blocks to the site by oxcart, lift the blocks into place, and fix them in concrete mortar. It took ten to fifteen years of backbreaking work to complete a large stone church. The final task of the padres was to arrange transportation of the religious art created in mainland studios across land and sea to the Baja missions for installation.

The great tragedy of the Baja California missionary adventure was that, soon after the stone churches were completed, the Native American converts, for whom they were built, died off from smallpox epidemics spread by their neighbors, the Spanish colonists. By 1840 the last surviving missions on the Baja California peninsula were abandoned by the priests and most of the colonizers. Churches built with sun-dried adobe bricks, being left to the forces of nature for a century or more, crumbled back to earth. The only original Spanish churches on Baja California to survive the ravages of time were eight stout buildings erected of stone. Some of these churches were cared for by the families who stayed on after the padres, hardy stragglers who eked out an existence from the land, eventually causing a few modern towns to rise from the dust of the old Spanish missions.

These days, Baja California's eight Spanish colonial churches receive constant attention from the Instituto Nacional de Antropología e Historia, as evidenced by ongoing structural improvements and careful restoration of the delicate artwork. Two current road-paving projects giving smoother, quicker access to San Javier and San José de Comondú missions demonstrate the importance of Baja's historic churches to the Mexican government and to the rural populace. There is no doubt that the Baja California missions embody a common source of pride for citizens of the peninsula. Annual fiestas commemorating the patron saint of each historic church are popular events that attract the local population as well as Mexican and American tourists.

A public church fiesta unites the community, bringing family, neighbors, and strangers from afar to celebrate mass, communion, and processions that honor the benevolent patron saint. These religious rituals, evidence that the Catholic Church still plays an important role in the lives of Baja Californians, provide moving experiences for the participants and for those who come to respectfully observe. There is plenty of entertainment: a carnival for the families, cowboy processions on horseback, matachín dancers that call up traditions of the extinct Indians. It's fun to dance to a *ranchera* band in the plaza, grill steaks at the campsite, fall asleep under the stars by a crackling bonfire.

When the eighteenth-century missions of Baja California are empty, which is most of the time, each sanctuary offers refuge in an atmosphere of peace and beauty. It feels good to rest inside the stone churches, to contemplate and pray, or just to observe the religious art. When you go to visit Baja's Spanish colonial missions, plan to camp overnight at one of the isolated locations. Take an evening stroll past the old church. As you walk in the footsteps of the padres, try to imagine what life was like at the Baja California missions two to three hundred years ago.

References

Aguilar Marco, José Luis, et al. *Misiones en la Península de Baja California.* Mexico City: Instituto Nacional de Antropología e Historia, 1991.

Arenas, Marco Antonio (hydrology engineer). Personal communication, Cabo San Lucas, Baja California Sur, 2006.

Baegert, Johann Jakob (Juan Jacobo). *Observations in Lower California.* Berkeley: University of California Press, 1952.

Cárdenas de la Peña, Enrique. *Urdaneta "El Tornaviaje."* Mexico City: Secretaría de Marina, 1965.

Clavijero, Francisco Xavier. *Historia de la antigua o Baja California.* Trans. Sara Lake. Stanford, CA: Stanford University Press, 1937.

Collier, Michael. *Land in Motion: California's San Andreas Fault.* Berkeley: University of California Press, 1999.

Crosby, Harry W. *Antigua California: Mission and Colony on the Colonial Frontier, 1697–1768.* Albuquerque: University of New Mexico Press, 1994.

de la Croix, Horst, and Richard G. Tansey. *Gardner's Art through the Ages.* New York: Harcourt Brace Jovanovich, 1986.

Engelhardt, Zephyrin. *The Missions and Missionaries of California,* vol. 1, *Lower California.* Santa Barbara, CA: Mission Santa Barbara, 1929.

Farmer, David Hugh. *Dictionary of Saints.* New York: Oxford University Press, 1997.

Fontana, Bernard L., and Edward McCain. *A Gift of Angels: The Art of Mission San Xavier del Bac.* Tucson: University of Arizona Press, 2010.

Jackson, Robert H. *Indian Population Decline.* Albuquerque: University of New Mexico Press, 1994.

———. "The 1781–1782 Small Pox Epidemic in Baja California." *Journal of California and Great Basin Anthropology* 3, no. 1 (1981): 138–42.

Mathes, W. Michael. *Las misiones de Baja California, 1683–1849.* La Paz, Baja California Sur: Editorial Aristos, 1977.

Meigs, Peveril. *The Dominican Mission Frontier of Lower California.* Berkeley: University of California Press, 1935.

Meyer de Stinglhamber, Bárbara. *Arte sacro en Baja California Sur—siglos XVII–XIX.* Mexico City: Instituto Nacional de Antropología e Historia, 2001.

Minor, Vernon Hyde. *Baroque and Rococo: Art and Culture.* London: Laurence King, 1999.

Olin, John C. *The Autobiography of St. Ignatius Loyola.* New York: Harper and Row, 1974.

O'Malley, John W. *The First Jesuits.* Cambridge, MA: Harvard University Press, 1995.

O'Malley, John W., et al. *The Jesuits: Cultures, Sciences and the Arts, 1540–1773.* Toronto: University of Toronto Press, 1999.

Pagden, Anthony. *Hernan Cortes: Letters from Mexico.* New Haven, CT: Yale University Press, 1986.

Palmerlee, Danny. *Baja and Los Cabos.* Victoria, Austral.: Lonely Planet, 2005.

Riney, Brad. *Plate Tectonics: How Baja California and the Sea of Cortez Were Formed.* Ocean Oasis Field Guide. San Diego: San Diego Natural History Museum, 2000.

Roberts, Norman C. *Baja California Plant Field Guide.* La Jolla, CA: Natural History Publishing Company, 1989.

Rodríguez de Montalvo, Garci. *The Labors of the Very Brave Knight Esplandián.* Trans. William Thomas Little. Binghamton, NY: Center for Medieval and Renaissance Texts and Studies, 1992.

Schuetz-Miller, Mardith K. "Pre-Euclidian Geometry in the Design of Mission Churches of the Spanish Borderlands." *Journal of the Southwest* 48, no. 4 (2006): 331–619.

Steinbeck, John. *The Log from the Sea of Cortez.* 1941; New York: Penguin Books, 1995.

Taraval, Sigismundo, and Marguerite Eyer Wilbur, trans. *The Indian Uprising in Lower California, 1734–1737.* Los Angeles: Quivira Society, 1931; New York: Arno Press, 1967.

Vernon, Edward W. *Las Misiones Antiguas: The Spanish Missions of Baja California.* Santa Barbara, CA: Viejo Press, 2002.

About the Authors

DAVID BURCKHALTER has spent many years photographing the Indians and rural people of Sonora, Mexico. In pursuit of his interest in Spanish colonial architecture and art, he plans to continue traveling in Mexico. David lives in Tucson, Arizona.

MINA (GUILLERMINA ARENAS) SEDGWICK was born and raised in Sonora, Mexico. Mina has traveled throughout Mexico, always with an interest in viewing religious art. A talented artist, she began taking photographs fifteen years ago. Mina lives on a ranch outside of Nogales, Arizona.

The Southwest Center Series

Joseph C. Wilder, Editor

Ignaz Pfefferkorn, *Sonora: A Description of the Province*

Carl Lumholtz, *New Trails in Mexico*

Buford Pickens, *The Missions of Northern Sonora: A 1935 Field Documentation*

Gary Paul Nabhan, editor, *Counting Sheep: Twenty Ways of Seeing Desert Bighorn*

Eileen Oktavec, *Answered Prayers: Miracles and Milagros along the Border*

Curtis M. Hinsley and David R. Wilcox, editors, *Frank Hamilton Cushing and the Hemenway Southwestern Archaeological Expedition, 1886–1889,* volume 1: *The Southwest in the American Imagination: The Writings of Sylvester Baxter, 1881–1899*

Lawrence J. Taylor and Maeve Hickey, *The Road to Mexico*

Donna J. Guy and Thomas E. Sheridan, editors, *Contested Ground: Comparative Frontiers on the Northern and Southern Edges of the Spanish Empire*

Julian D. Hayden, *The Sierra Pinacate*

Paul S. Martin, David Yetman, Mark Fishbein, Phil Jenkins, Thomas R. Van Devender, and Rebecca K. Wilson, editors, *Gentry's Rio Mayo Plants: The Tropical Deciduous Forest and Environs of Northwest Mexico*

W J McGee, *Trails to Tiburón: The 1894 and 1895 Field Diaries of W J McGee,* transcribed by Hazel McFeely Fontana, annotated and with an introduction by Bernard L. Fontana

Richard Stephen Felger, *Flora of the Gran Desierto and Río Colorado of Northwestern Mexico*

Donald Bahr, editor, *O'odham Creation and Related Events: As Told to Ruth Benedict in 1927 in Prose, Oratory, and Song by the Pimas William Blackwater, Thomas Vanyiko, Clara Ahiel, William Stevens, Oliver Wellington, and Kisto*

Dan L. Fischer, *Early Southwest Ornithologists, 1528–1900*

Thomas Bowen, editor, *Backcountry Pilot: Flying Adventures with Ike Russell*

Federico José María Ronstadt, *Borderman: Memoirs of Federico José María Ronstadt,* edited by Edward F. Ronstadt

Curtis M. Hinsley and David R. Wilcox, editors, *Frank Hamilton Cushing and the Hemenway Southwestern Archaeological Expedition, 1886–1889,* volume 2: *The Lost Itinerary of Frank Hamilton Cushing*

Neil Goodwin, *Like a Brother: Grenville Goodwin's Apache Years, 1928–1939*

Katherine G. Morrissey and Kirsten Jensen, editors, *Picturing Arizona: The Photographic Record of the 1930s*

Bill Broyles and Michael Berman, *Sunshot: Peril and Wonder in the Gran Desierto*

David W. Lazaroff, Philip C. Rosen, and Charles H. Lowe Jr., *Amphibians, Reptiles, and Their Habitats at Sabino Canyon*

David Yetman, *The Organ Pipe Cactus*

Gloria Fraser Giffords, *Sanctuaries of Earth, Stone, and Light: The Churches of Northern New Spain, 1530–1821*

David Yetman, *The Great Cacti: Ethnobotany and Biogeography*

John Messina, *Álamos, Sonora: Architecture and Urbanism in the Dry Tropics*

Laura L. Cummings, *Pachucas and Pachucos in Tucson: Situated Border Lives*

Bernard L. Fontana and Edward McCain, *A Gift of Angels: The Art of Mission San Xavier del Bac*

David A. Yetman, *The Ópatas: In Search of a Sonoran People*

Julian D. Hayden, *Field Man: The Life of a Desert Archaeologist*, edited by Bill Broyles and Diane Boyer

Thomas E. Sheridan, *Arizona: A History*, Revised Edition

Bill Broyles, Gayle Harrison Hartmann, Thomas E. Sheridan, Gary Paul Nabhan, and Mary Charlotte Thurtle, *Last Water on the Devil's Highway: A Cultural and Natural History of Tinajas Altas*

Richard Stephen Felger and Benjamin Theodore Wilder, in collaboration with Humberto Romero-Morales, *Plant Life of a Desert Archipelago: Flora of the Sonoran Islands in the Gulf of California*

David Burckhalter and Mina Sedgwick, *Baja California Missions: In the Footsteps of the Padres*

Index